Netherland Dwarf Rabbits

This publication is Copyright 2013 by EKL Publishing. All products, publications, software and services mentioned and recommended in this publication are protected by trademarks. In such instance, all trademarks & copyright belong to the respective owners.

The moral rights of the author has been asserted

British Library Cataloguing in Publication Data

A catalogue record for this book is available from the British Library
ISBN 978-1-909820-19-7

Disclaimer and Legal Notice

Netherland Dwarf Rabbits

The Complete Owner's Guide to

Netherland Dwarf Bunnies

How to Care for your Netherland Dwarf, including
Health, Breeding, Lifespan, Colors, Diet, Facts and Clubs

Foreword

Hello and thank you for buying my book.

In this book you will find some wonderful information to help you care for your Netherland Dwarf Rabbit. I've included in this book information about their care, habitat, cages, enclosure, diet, facts, set up, names, pictures, life span, breeding, feeding, cost and a care sheet. After reading this book you will be a lot more confident in looking after your Netherland Dwarf Rabbit!

I have written this book using American spelling as that is what I'm used to. I have given measurements in both feet and inches/pounds and ounces and also in metric. I have also given costs in US$ and GBP. Both the measurements and costs are approximate guides. I have done my best to ensure the accuracy of the information in this book as at the time of publishing.

I trust that after reading this book you will enjoy the experience of owning and looking after a Netherland Dwarf Rabbit and that you have a wonderful time enjoying the pleasure they bring in the years to come!

All good wishes, Ann L. Fletcher

Acknowledgements

I would like to thank my daughter Stacey for sharing with me her experiences of living with her Netherland Dwarf rabbit, Millie who has brought lots of fun and enjoyment to her family. It's always wonderful to share a passion with your children and I love that another generation has gone on to experience the delight these wonderful creatures bring. Her granddad would be so proud.

My love and thanks to my husband John for his patience and understanding over the years. I couldn't have done it without him.

Table of Contents

Chapter One: Introduction

T he Netherland Dwarf Rabbit is a very small breed (as implied by its name) and one of the most popular breeds for show. These rabbits are known for their infantile physical traits as well as their varied coat colors and patterns. Aside from their physical characteristics, the docile and friendly nature of this breed also plays a role in their popularity. If you are looking for a good family pet, the Netherland Dwarf Rabbit is certainly one to consider.

Weighing in at an average of 2 lbs (0.91 kg) when young, these rabbits are one of the smallest breeds of rabbits. Despite their small size, they do require as much space and care as any other rabbit breed. Like all rabbits, Netherland Dwarfs require a healthy diet and plenty of space to stretch out and hop around. If you are not able to provide your rabbit with these basic necessities, a Netherland Dwarf is not the right choice for you.

In this book you have a superb resource for much of the information you need to prepare and care for your Netherland Dwarf Rabbit. From the basics about this breed in general to details for feeding, housing and breeding, this book is a comprehensive guide for new and experienced rabbit owners alike. Within the pages of this book you will find the extensive knowledge necessary to help you properly care for your Netherland Dwarf Rabbits – maybe even the answers to some questions you didn't even know you had!

Useful Terms to Know:

- **Buck**: a male rabbit

- **Cross Breeding**: breeding two different breeds together

- **Crown**: refers to a prominent ridge and crest along the top of the head extending to the base of the ears

- **Dam**: the mother of a rabbit

- **Doe**: a female rabbit

- **Hock**: the joint of the rabbit's foot

- **Inbreeding**: breeding two closely related rabbits to each other (e.g. brother to sister)

- **Junior**: young rabbit between 14 weeks and 5 months

- **Kindling**: process of giving birth to a litter of kits

- **Kit**: a baby rabbit

- **Litter**: two or more baby rabbits resulting from a single pregnancy/kindling

- **Lopped**: pendulous ears (opposite of erect ears)

- **Stud Buck**: a male rabbit suitable for breeding

- **Sire**: the father of a rabbit

- **Weaning**: the process through which kits begin to eat more solid food and rely less on nursing

Chapter Two: Understanding Them

Before you go out and buy a Netherland Dwarf rabbit, you would be wise to learn a little bit about the breed. While all pet rabbit breeds are descendant from the domestic rabbit, different breeds have different personalities and requirements for care. In order to properly care for your rabbit you need to learn about this specific breed so you can provide the right environment, diet and care. In this chapter you will learn some key facts about the Netherland Dwarf as a breed.

1.) What Are Netherland Dwarf Rabbits?

The Netherland Dwarf is a breed of domestic rabbit (Oryctolagus cuniculus) that has become very popular as a pet. These rabbits remain fairly small, as suggested by the "dwarf" part of their name. Generally, mature Netherland Dwarfs weigh no more than 3.5 lbs (1.59 kg). These little rabbits are kept both as pets and exhibition animals, but they are not typically raised for meat or fur due to their diminutive size.

These rabbits are one of the most popular breeds for rabbit shows. In fact, most rabbits shown at rabbit shows are either Netherland Dwarfs or derived from the Netherland Dwarf breed. Perhaps what makes this breed so popular is their small size and baby-like appearance. Even though they are very small, however, these rabbits can be very active and entertaining as pets.

It is important to realize that, despite their size, Netherland Dwarf rabbits do require a significant amount of space. You should also be aware that Netherland Dwarfs have a reputation for being a rather shy and skittish breed – through years of selective breeding however, rabbit breeders have been able to develop the Netherland Dwarf into a generally docile breed. Though the disposition of each rabbit may vary, this breed is typically good with children and they are very hardy as household pets.

The key to keeping a Netherland Dwarf rabbit healthy is to provide a clean, safe environment and a healthy diet. Like most rabbits, Netherland Dwarfs require a vegetable based diet made up of 70-80% grass or hay. They should also be given commercial rabbit pellets to fill in the gaps in their diet as well as the occasional fresh vegetable. If you provide the proper care for your rabbit, you can easily enjoy its company for 5 to 10 years – maybe more!

In this book you will learn a wealth of information about the Netherland Dwarf breed so you can provide the optimal care for your rabbit.

2.) Facts about Netherland Dwarf Rabbits

As you've already learned, the Netherland Dwarf is a breed of domestic rabbit. It is known for its small size and baby-like appearance as well as its popularity for show. What gives these rabbits their baby-like appearance is the fact that their head and eyes are disproportionately large compared to the rest of the body. These rabbits have rounded, short faces and a compact, well-rounded body.

These particular features can be attributed to dwarfism, a medical condition that is genetically inherited in this breed.

Netherland Dwarf rabbits can be either purebred or some type of cross. These rabbits can be crossed with other breeds and, depending on the breed used; it may affect the rabbit's physical characteristics. Purebred Netherland Dwarfs, however, retain their infantile characteristics and they come in a variety of colors including:

Black	Chestnut
Blue	Sable
Chocolate	Chinchilla
Himalayan	Tortoiseshell
Lilac	Sable Point
Smoke Pearl	Opal
Lynx	Silver Marten
Tan	Otter
Squirrel	Sable Marten
Orange	Fawn
Steel	Broken
Blue-Eyed White	Ruby-Eyed White

Generally, full-grown Netherland Dwarf rabbits range from 1.1 to 3.5 lbs (0.5 to 1.59 kg) in weight. Ideal show weight, however, is about 2 lbs (0.91 kg). These rabbits have erect ears that measure up to 2 inches (5.08 centimeters) long and a soft, dense coat that rolls off the back. The front legs are short and straight and the overall appearance of the body is compact and cobby (round with very small neck).

Summary of Facts

Species: domestic rabbit, (Oryctolagus cuniculus)
Classification: dwarf breed
Weight: 1.1 to 3.5 lbs. (0.5 to 1.59 kg)
Body Shape: short, compact and rounded
Body Structure: cobby, full-chested and wide-shouldered
Coat: soft, short and dense
Coat Color: 36 show colors accepted by ARBA, divided into 5 groups
Lifespan: average 5 to 10 years

3.) History of Netherland Dwarf Rabbits as Pets

The origins of this breed can be traced all the way back to the 1800s in the Netherlands. During the 1800s, multiple litters of Dutch rabbits were born with kits exhibiting white coats, red eyes and cobby bodies. These specimens were called "Polish" rabbits and were selectively bred to develop the breed. This new breed was first exhibited in Hull, England in 1884 and was soon after exported to Germany where it was greeted with enthusiasm.

In Germany, a standard for the breed was created which is similar to the standard for today's modern Netherland Dwarf. White "Polish" rabbits were crossed with small wild rabbits to improve the type and, over time, new colors were introduced into the bloodline. During the 1930s, a Dutch fancier named Jan Meyering and some of his associates began to cross the "Polish" breed with other breeds. By 1940, a new line of colored dwarfs had emerged and was soon given its own breed standard.

The Netherland Dwarf, as the new breed came to be called, was introduced to the United States of America in 1965. In 1969, Darrell Bramhall began to improve and develop the breed and eventually appeared before the American Rabbit Breeders Association (ARBA) to request New Breed status. The ARBA recognized the Netherland Dwarf and approved a breed standard based on the standard written by the British Rabbit Council (BRC).

Early specimens of the breed exhibited fearful or aggressive temperaments. This largely came about due to crossbreeding with small wild rabbits for their size.

Through selective breeding, however, the Netherland Dwarf came to be gentle and friendly, though many exhibit higher energy levels than larger domestic breeds.

a.) History of the British Rabbit Council

The breeding and showing of rabbits began over two hundred years ago. Throughout the nineteenth century, fanciers gathered to form local clubs for showing and improving individual breeds. The number of rabbit breeds recognized increased throughout the 1800s and early 1900s but by 1918, the most popular breed by far was the Beveren. In May of 1918 breeders of Beveren rabbits gathered to form a national club called The Beveren Club.

The Beveren Club served to raise the profile of rabbit breeding, adopting and standardizing new breeds. Eventually, the name of the club changed to the British Fur Rabbit Society and then to the British Rabbit Society. By 1928, over a dozen different breeds were recognized and interest in rabbit breeding began to grow. As a result, a new club was formed called the National Rabbit Council of Great Britain. The club grew quickly but conflicts arose between the two clubs which led to them eventually merging in 1934 to form the British Rabbit Council (BRC).

b.) History of the American Rabbit Breeders Association

The American Rabbit Breeders Association (ARBA) was founded in 1910 and has its headquarters in Bloomington, Illinois. The purpose of this association is to promote rabbit fancy and to facilitate commercial rabbit production. The ARBA is responsible for setting breed standards and sanctioning rabbit shows throughout North America. In addition to sponsoring local clubs and fairs, the ARBA holds a national convention show annually, drawing rabbit fanciers from around the globe.

Not only does the ARBA set breed standards and organize shows, it also serves to provide rabbit raising education. Every five years the ARBA publishes a detailed guide for rabbit fanciers called Standard of Perfection. The ARBA also publishes educational materials like guidebooks and posters including photographs of all the recognized rabbit breeds. Additionally, the ARBA has a library of over 10,000 books and writings on domestic rabbits – the largest single repository of its kind.

Chapter Three: What to Know Before You Buy

There are a few key things you should think about before you go out and buy a Netherland Dwarf Rabbit. First, is it legal to keep these rabbits as pets in your area? Are there any restrictions as to the number you can keep or whether you breed them? You should also find out whether it is better to keep Netherland Dwarfs singularly or in pairs – if you have other pets at home, you also need to make sure they are compatible. In this chapter you will find all the basic information you need to know before buying a Netherland Dwarf Rabbit.

1.) Do You Need a License?

Now that you've learned the basics about this wonderful breed you can move on to thinking about what you need to do before you buy your Netherland Dwarf Rabbits. Before you even start to think about where you are going to get your rabbit you need to determine whether you are required to have a license or permit to keep rabbits as pets in your area.

a.) Licensing in the U.S.A.

There is no federal law in the United States of America requiring private rabbit owners to obtain a license for keeping Netherland Dwarf Rabbits. There are, however, certain state laws regarding the keeping and breeding of domestic rabbits. The state of Minnesota, for example, requires rabbit owners to pay a $15 annual fee to license their pet rabbit – a higher fee may be charged if the rabbit is not spayed or neutered.

Generally, retail pet store owners and private collectors are not required to obtain a permit for keeping Netherland Dwarf Rabbits. If you plan to breed your rabbits for wholesale or exhibition, however, you may need to obtain a license. To determine the requirements for your particular area, check with your local council. It is better to be safe than sorry – especially if failing to license your rabbit could cost you hefty fines.

b.) Licensing in the U.K.

The U.K. does not have any legislation requiring rabbit owners or breeders to obtain a license. There are, however, laws in place in regard to importing or exporting animals. Rabies has long been eradicated from the U.K. and strict import and export laws are now in place to prevent the disease from being re-introduced. If you plan to bring a rabbit with you to the U.K., or if you plan to export one, you will need to obtain an animal movement license (AML).

c.) Licensing Elsewhere

Licensing requirements for Netherland Dwarf Rabbits vary from one country or region to another. One of the only cases in which the ownership of pet rabbits is expressly prohibited is in Queensland, Australia. Rabbits are not a native species in Queensland – they are actually considered a Class 2 pest by the Land Protection Act of 2002. A penalty of Australian $44,000 can be levied as a result of flaunting this law.

As they are not a native species, rabbits can threaten the survival of certain native species and also cause damage to the environment. You cannot obtain a license to keep a pet rabbit in Queensland because it is illegal. The only time in which a permit may be issued is if the rabbit is being used for research or entertainment purposes.

2.) How Many Should You Buy?

Most rabbits are very social creatures by nature. This being the case, many inexperienced rabbit owners assume that it is best to keep them with others of their own kind. The fact that Netherland Dwarfs can be gentle with humans does not necessarily mean they are a social breed. In fact, Netherland Dwarf Rabbits do not need to be kept in pairs or in groups – they simply need a regular amount of daily interaction in order to thrive.

Keeping more than one rabbit in the same living space can be tricky. While Netherland Dwarfs are friendly and gentle creatures by nature, you can never know for sure how a rabbit will react to another rabbit entering its territory. In the wild, rabbit colonies tend to form a strict hierarchy and they have been known to defend their territory. If you try to keep two rabbits together and one is more dominant than the other, the subservient rabbit could become stressed and fall ill due to the bullying of the other rabbit.

If you truly want to form a close bond with your rabbit, it is best to keep only one. Your rabbit doesn't need another rabbit companion as long as you give it plenty of love and attention yourself. In fact, your rabbit is more likely to bond with you if you do not keep it with another rabbit. If, however, you do want to keep more than one rabbit together it is best to buy them when they are the same age so they can be raised together. It is not a good idea to add a new rabbit to an already established cage – this is likely to cause territorial issues.

3.) Can They Be Kept with Other Pets?

Like most rabbit breeds, Netherland Dwarf Rabbits are very gentle and playful by nature. This being the case, these rabbits can generally be kept with other pets. If you plan to keep your rabbit with other household pets it is important that you socialize your rabbit properly and supervise the time your rabbit spends with other pets. While your other pets may not be aggressive by nature, animal behavior is difficult to predict and it is always better to be safe than sorry.

My best advice is not to take any chances but ultimately you must make a judgment call as you are best placed to know the character of your pets.

Follow these tips when keeping a Netherland Dwarf Rabbit in the same house as other pets:

- Make sure your rabbit has a safe place to retreat to if it wants to

- Always supervise your Netherland Dwarf's time with other pets to prevent accidents

- Do not keep Netherland Dwarfs with ferrets – ferrets are predatory animals and may injure your rabbit

- Netherland Dwarfs can bond with a variety of pets including cats, dogs and guinea pigs

- Prevent your rabbit from accessing the food of other pets (cats, dogs, etc.)

- If you have pets kept in tanks (e. g. fish and frogs), please ensure that they do not chew on electrical cords. This would obviously apply to any electrical cords throughout your home.

- Rabbits may not get along with birds – due to their sensitive ears, noisy birds may irritate rabbits

4.) Ease and Cost of Care

Netherland Dwarf Rabbits are an excellent choice for a family pet because they are gentle, friendly and love to have the attention of their human companions. Before you go out and buy a rabbit, however, you should be sure that you can handle the initial and monthly costs. The initial costs of a Netherland Dwarf Rabbit include the purchase price of the rabbit itself plus the cost of spay/neuter surgery, microchipping and initial vaccinations as well as the cost of the cage and accessories. Once you cover these costs you must also think about monthly costs such as food, bedding and veterinary care. Think about all of these costs before you decide to buy a Netherland Dwarf Rabbit.

a.) Initial Costs

Purchase Price: The price of a Netherland Dwarf Rabbit will vary depending where you buy it. You may be able to find these rabbits at your local pet store for around $20 to $30 (£13 to £19.50). These rabbits are not guaranteed to be pedigreed, however. Pedigreed Netherland Dwarf Rabbits bred for show tend to be more expensive than other rabbits – they can cost as much as $40 to $60 (£26 to £39).

Spay/Neuter: If you do not plan to breed your rabbits, it is normally a good idea to spay or neuter them. The cost of the spay/neuter surgery is generally around $100 (£65) but you may be able to find a lower price if there is a veterinary clinic in your area. Seek advice from your vet of the pros and cons of having your rabbit spayed or neutered.

Microchipping: A microchip is a tiny electronic device that is inserted under your rabbit's skin. This device is used to store your contact information so if the rabbit is lost, you can be contacted. It is not a requirement that you have your rabbit microchipped, but it is certainly a good idea. The cost of this procedure is generally about $30 (£19.50).

Vaccinations: One of the first things you need to do when you get a new rabbit is to have it examined by a veterinarian and caught up on its vaccinations. Costs for veterinary care may vary depending where you live but the average cost for initial vaccinations is around $50 to $65 (£32.50 to £42.25).

Cage: Netherland Dwarf Rabbits are a very small breed, weighing a maximum of 3.5 lbs (1.59 kg) at maturity. This being the case, they do not require a very large cage. It is important, however, that you provide your rabbits with plenty of space to hop around and stretch out. You may also choose to let your rabbit roam free throughout the house. Even if you do that, you should have a cage or hutch where your rabbit can sleep at night. The cost for a rabbit's cage will vary depending on size and materials, but you should be ready to spend around $200 to $300 (£130 - £195).

Accessories: To prepare your rabbit's cage you will need to stock up on a few accessories. These accessories might include a water bottle, food bowl, bedding and chew toys for your rabbit. Another accessory that would be good to have around is a travel carrier – this will be useful when you need to take your rabbit to the vet. The cost of initial accessories may be around $100 (£65).

Additional Costs: In addition to purchasing your rabbit as well as his cage and accessories, there are a few additional costs you should be prepared for. Some of these costs might include a litter pan, grooming supplies and cleaning equipment. For the most part, these tools and supplies should last you for several years and the total cost may average around $100 (£65).

Summary of Initial Costs

Cost Type	One Rabbit	Two Rabbits
Purchase Price	$20 - $60 (£13 - £39)	$40 to $120 (£26 - £78)
Spay/Neuter	$100 (£65)	$200 (£130)
Microchipping	$30 (£19.50)	$60 (£39)
Vaccinations	$50 to $65 (£32.50 to £42.25)	$100 to $130 (£65 to £84.50)
Cage or Pen	$200 to $300 (£130 to £195)	$200 to $300 (£130 - £195)
Cage Accessories	$100 (£65)	$100 (£65)
Other Tools/Equipment	$100 (£65)	$100 (£65)
Total:	$600 - $755 (£390 - £490.75)	$800 - $1,010 (£520 - £656.50)

b.) Monthly Costs

In addition to these initial costs, you should also be ready to pay for several other costs on a monthly basis. In order to

properly care for your Netherland Dwarf Rabbit you will
need to buy fresh food and bedding every month – you
may also need to provide routine or emergency veterinary
care. You should also be prepared to pay for additional
costs such as replacing accessories or making repairs to the
cage. Below you will find an explanation of the monthly
costs you can come to expect as a Netherland Dwarf Rabbit
owner.

Food: Your monthly costs for rabbit food will vary
depending how many rabbits you keep and what type of
food you buy. Some of the types of food you will need to
buy for your rabbits include greens, hay, commercial rabbit
pellets and fresh vegetables. The cost to feed a single
Netherland Dwarf Rabbit for one month averages about $30
(£19.50).

Bedding: If you plan to keep your rabbit in its cage or
hutch, your bedding costs may be higher than if you let
your rabbit roam free throughout the house. Your monthly
cost for bedding will also depend on the type of bedding
you buy. In general, you should plan to spend up to $50
(£32.50) per month on bedding. You can reduce your
bedding costs by using recycled newspapers, but do not use
colored magazines because the ink may contain toxins that
are harmful to your rabbit.

Veterinary Care: If you care for your Netherland Dwarf properly, you should not have to worry about veterinary care on a monthly basis. You should however, take your rabbit to the vet for a check-up once a year. The total yearly cost for this is generally around $50 (£32.50) which is less than $5 (£3.25) per month. However, you cannot predict veterinary expenses if your rabbit becomes unexpectedly ill and should have savings for this or could consider pet insurance. Please see Chapter Six for more details.

Additional Costs: Other monthly costs you should be prepared for include replacing chew toys and making repairs to the cage or supplies. These costs are generally not very high and may only be $30 (£19.50) per year which is $2.50 (£1.63) per month.

Summary of Monthly Costs

Cost Type	One Rabbit	Two Rabbits
Food	$30 (£19.50)	$60 (£39)
Bedding	$50 (£32.50)	$50 (£32.50)
Veterinary Care	$5 (£3.25)	$10 (£6.50)
Additional Costs	$2.50 (£1.63)	$5 (£3.25)
Total:	$87.50 (£56.88)	$125 (£81.25)

c.) Time Considerations

In addition to the initial and monthly costs for keeping Netherland Dwarf rabbits, you also need to think about the amount of care these animals require and the time that this will take. Though Netherland Dwarf rabbits are not difficult to keep as pets, they do require regular maintenance. Refer to the following lists to get an idea how much time you will need to dedicate to your rabbit's care on a daily and weekly basis:

Daily Tasks to Complete:

- Clean food dish and refresh food

- Clean water bottle and refresh water

- Moving rabbit to exercise pen (20 to 30 minutes daily)

- Interacting with the rabbit

- Observation/basic health check

Estimated Daily Commitment: 1 hour

Weekly Tasks to Complete:

- Completely replacing bedding
- Cleaning out cage and accessories
- More detailed health check
- Spending extended time interacting with rabbit
- Checking ears, nails and teeth
- Combing/brushing rabbit (when molting you may need to do this daily)

Estimated Weekly Commitment: *10 hours*

5.) Human Health Considerations

Before you buy you also need to consider any implications to your own health. For example, do you know if you have an allergy or sensitivity to rabbits? I would recommendation taking advice from your Doctor to ensure that you understand that implications to your own health and if necessary, are allergy tested.

6.) Pros and Cons of Netherland Dwarf Rabbits

Choosing the right breed of rabbit for you and your family can be difficult. To help you make your decision, consult this list of pros and cons for Netherland Dwarf Rabbits. Many of these pros and cons apply to keeping any rabbit as a pet, but some are specific to the Netherland Dwarf breed.

Pros for Netherland Dwarf Rabbits

- Very friendly and playful as a breed, good family pet

- Small breed

- Come in a wide variety of colors – very attractive appearance

- Can be trained to perform simple tricks and respond to commands

- Very quiet compared to other pet breeds

- Docile personality – can get along with cats, dogs and other household pets

- The Netherland Dwarf is easy to litter train – makes clean-up and cage maintenance easier

- Breed tends to bond closely with humans, makes them a good companion pet

Cons for Netherland Dwarf Rabbits

- May be slightly less social than larger breeds, requires plenty of socialization

- Require plenty of human attention and interaction, may not be recommended for inexperienced owners

- Temperament may vary depending on the animal, not all Netherland Dwarfs are gentle by nature

- Needs a lot of chew toys to keep teeth from becoming overgrown

- Not necessarily a low-maintenance pet, need just as much care as a dog or cat

- Fairly fragile as a pet, not recommended for boisterous or young children

- May become destructive if allowed to roam freely – will chew on cords and furniture

- May begin to display aggressive/territorial behavior once they reach breeding age

- Odor can be unpleasant if kept indoors and not cleaned often enough

Chapter Four: Purchasing Your Rabbit

I f you've decided that a Netherland Dwarf really is the right breed for you, you might be ready to think about buying one. Buying a rabbit can be a tricky process because you don't want to spend too much money but you want to get a rabbit that has been bred well. In this chapter you will find tips for finding a healthy rabbit in both the U.S.A. and the U.K.

1.) Where to Buy Netherland Dwarf Rabbits

When it comes to buying Netherland Dwarf Rabbits, you have several options to choose from. As this breed is not one of the most common, you may not be able to find them in your local pet store as they might carry only a few selected breeds. If you plan to breed your rabbits or train them for show, you should plan to purchase from an independent breeder anyway. For those who simply want a Netherland Dwarf Rabbit as a pet, another excellent option is to adopt a rabbit from your local rabbit rescue group.

a.) Buying in the U.S.A.

In the United States of America, you may be able to find Netherland Dwarf Rabbits at your local pet store depending on how large a selection they have. Keep in mind, however, that rabbits sold at pet stores may not be bred from high-quality stock and they may be more likely to be exposed to disease. Even if you do not buy from the pet store, you may still be able to get information about local breeders in your area. You might also try asking your veterinarian for a referral.

Another option is to perform an online search for Netherland Dwarf Rabbit breeders. You can often find

listings of breeders on national websites such as the
American Rabbit Breeders Association. If all else fails, look
for a rabbit rescue in your area. You may not find a rescue
that has baby rabbits available, but adult rabbits are likely
to already be litter trained and are more likely to be caught
up on vaccinations. If you want a pet, it is great to be able to
give a rescue rabbit a good home.

U.S.A. Breeder Websites:

American Netherland Dwarf Rabbit Club Breeders List:
www.andrc.com/Breeders.php

ARBA Breeder Listing: www.arba.net/breeders.htm

Netherland Dwarf Rabbit Breeders:
http://rabbitbreeders.us/netherland-dwarf-rabbit-breeders

You may also be able to find Netherland Dwarf Rabbits at a
rabbit rescue in your area. Try these websites to adopt a
rabbit:

Florida Rabbit Rescue: http://rabbit.rescueme.org/Florida

Right Pet: www.rightpet.com/small-exotic-
mammalrescues/adoption-rescue/netherland-dwarf-rabbit

Heartland Rabbit Rescue: www.heartlandrabbitrescue.org/

b.) Buying in the U.K.

Depending on the selection of breeds kept, you might be able to find Netherland Dwarf Rabbits at your local pet store in the U.K. As is true in the U.S.A., you should be aware that rabbits sold at pet stores may not be bred from high-quality stock. If you don't want to buy from a pet store, ask your veterinarian or fellow rabbit owners for a referral to a breeder. Another option is to check the breeder listings on the British Rabbit Council or National Netherland Dwarf Rabbit Club websites.

U.K. Breeder Websites:

The British Rabbit Council Breeders Directory:
www.thebrc.org/breeders-list.htm

Netherland Dwarf Rabbit Breeders:
http://rabbitbreeders.org.uk/netherland-dwarf-rabbit-breeders

Scottish Netherland Dwarf Club Breeders List:
www.scottishnetherlanddwarf.co.uk/Contact%20Breeders.htm

You may also be able to find Netherland Dwarf Rabbits at a rabbit rescue in your area. Try these websites to adopt a rabbit:

Preloved:www.preloved.co.uk/adverts/list/3659/rabbits.html?keyword=netherland%20dwarf

Rabbit Rehome UK: www.rabbitrehome.org.uk/

The Rabbit Residence Rescue: www.rabbitresidence.org.uk

2.) How to Select a Healthy Netherland Dwarf Rabbit

Owning and caring for a Netherland Dwarf Rabbit is more than just a responsibility – it is a privilege. These creatures are an absolute joy to have around and, as the owner; it is your duty to keep your rabbit happy and healthy. In order to keep your Netherland Dwarf Rabbit healthy, you need to make sure it is healthy before you even bring it home.

Many inexperienced rabbit owners make the mistake of not taking the time to carefully select a breeder and to examine the rabbit before buying to make sure it is in good condition. In this section you will learn how to choose a reputable breeder and how to then pick out a healthy rabbit.

Follow these tips to make sure you bring home a healthy Netherland Dwarf Rabbit:

Do your research: Shop around for a reputable breeder and take the time to interview each breeder. Ask questions to ascertain the breeder's knowledge of and experience with the Netherland Dwarf Breed. If the breeder can't answer your questions or appears to be avoiding them, move on to another breeder.

Ask for a tour: Once you select a breeder, pay a visit to the facilities. Ask to see the places where the rabbits are kept and ask to see the parents of the litter from which you are buying. If the facilities are dirty or the parents appear to be in poor health, do not purchase a rabbit from that breeder.

Observe the kits: If the facilities and parents appear to be in good order, ask to see the litter of rabbits. Observe their appearance and activity to see if they look healthy. Healthy Netherland Dwarfs should be active and curious, not hiding in a corner or looking lethargic.

Examine the rabbits individually: If the litter appears to be in good condition, pick out a few of the rabbits that you like. Handle the rabbits briefly to see how they react to human interaction and check them for obvious signs of disease and injury. Check the rabbit's ears and nose for discharge and make sure that the eyes are bright and clear. The rabbit's teeth should be straight and its coat healthy.

If, after touring the facilities and ensuring that the rabbits themselves are healthy, you can begin to make negotiations with the breeder. Make sure you get the rabbit's medical history and breeding information for your own records. Ask if the rabbit comes with a health guarantee and make sure you get all the paperwork necessary to register your rabbit, should you choose to do so.

Chapter Five: Caring for your Rabbit

Owning a Netherland Dwarf Rabbit brings much happiness and with it responsibility. As such, it is imperative that you provide your rabbit with the best care possible – this includes the right habitat, a healthy diet, and any other needs your rabbit may have. In this chapter you will find all the information you need to properly care for your Netherland Dwarf Rabbit.

1.) Habitat Requirements

Though they are a dwarf breed, Netherland Dwarf Rabbits do require a fairly significant amount of space for their size. These rabbits can be very active so they need room to stretch out and hop around. Many rabbit owners choose to let their rabbits roam freely throughout the house during the day, providing them with a cage to sleep in at night. No matter what you choose to do with your Netherland Dwarf Rabbit, you need to think carefully about the type of habitat you provide for your new pet. If your rabbit isn't given the proper environment, he may fail to thrive.

a.) Tips for Netherland Dwarf Cages

One of the best options for Netherland Dwarf Rabbits is an open exercise pen or rabbit run. An open exercise pen or rabbit run can be as large as you like but the walls should be at least 3 feet (0.91 meters) high so your bunny doesn't escape. You can easily build a pen for your rabbit in a spare bedroom in your house using attachable wire cubes – you can even convert a puppy pen into a run for your rabbit. Another option is to keep your rabbit in a cage but provide it with an outdoor run for additional exercise. If you choose to build an outdoor rabbit run, be sure to bury the wire at least a few inches/centimeters underground to prevent your rabbit from digging under it. Please also make sure the top of the pen is covered so predators cannot get in to attack your rabbit. Another thing you need to think about when keeping your rabbit in an exercise pen outdoors is that you should cover about half of the pen with a towel or another solid object to provide your rabbit with shade.

In terms of an indoor cage, it is important to remember that your Netherland Dwarf Rabbit is going to spend a significant amount of time in this cage - it is essential that you pick a good one. As I said earlier, though these rabbits do remain fairly small, they still need to have plenty of space in their cage. A cage for Netherland Dwarfs should be long enough that your rabbit can make three or four hops from one end to the other. The cage should be wide enough that your rabbit can stretch out across the width and tall enough that it can stand on its hind legs.

In addition to the size, you also need to think about the materials from which your rabbit cage is built. Metal cages made from wire mesh with a solid bottom are best. Cages that have wire mesh bottoms may make clean-up easier by allowing feces to fall through the holes, but it can also hurt your rabbit's feet. It is far better to clean out your rabbit's cage often enough that the bedding remains fresh. The thing to keep in mind with solid-bottom cages is that if you do not clean them out often enough, the dampness from the bedding could make your rabbit ill.

In terms of bedding, the best kinds to use are non-toxic pelleted litter, fresh hay or newspaper. Pine and cedar shavings can cause irritation and both clay and clumping cat litters can be harmful to rabbits. You should also avoid using colored magazine pages as bedding because the ink on the pages may be toxic – it could be dangerous for your rabbit if he eats it. No matter what type of bedding you choose, be sure to replace it often even if it doesn't look like it needs it.

b.) Indoors or Outdoors?

Many inexperienced rabbit owners have a hard time deciding whether to keep their pet rabbits indoors or outdoors. If you have ever visited a farm, you might have seen rabbits in hutches – though it is fairly common to keep rabbits outdoors, it is not necessarily the best option. Whether you keep your Netherland Dwarf Rabbit indoors or outdoors is your choice, but you would be wise to learn the pros and cons of both options before you make a decision.

Benefits of Indoors vs. Outdoors:

Advantages of Indoor Rabbits

- More likely to form a bond with owners
- Less likely to come into contact with parasites
- Not exposed to inclement weather or predators
- More likely to receive adequate attention and interaction with human caregivers
- Longer lifespan, less susceptible to disease

Advantages of Outdoor Rabbits

- More space for rabbits to stretch out and exercise
- Clean-up can be much easier, may not even need to litter train rabbits
- Odor and noise are not an issue
- Easier to accommodate large cages and multiple rabbits
- In rabbit runs, rabbits can eat grass and other plants (which can also be a disadvantage if poisonous)

Disadvantages of Indoors vs. Outdoors:

Cons for Indoor Rabbits

- Free-roaming rabbits may chew on electrical cords, furniture, etc.

- Cage takes up space in the home

- Noise and odor is more noticeable if cage isn't cleaned often enough

- Free-roaming rabbits may be underfoot – could potentially be injured

Cons for Outdoor Rabbits

- May be less likely to form a bond with human caretakers and pets as rabbits may not receive as much human interaction

- More likely to be exposed to parasites and other dangerous diseases

- At risk for attack by predators

- May be exposed to inclement weather and extreme temperatures

c.) Multi-level vs. Single-Level Cages

You will need to think about what type of cage you want to use. There are a number of different types of rabbit cages but the major distinctions are between single-level and multi-level cages. Multi-level cages are also referred to as rabbit condos and they provide vertical space as well as horizontal space. Single-level cages are exactly what they sound like – cages that provide space on one level.

The main difference between these two options is the amount of space they provide. With a single-level cage, the only way to provide more space is to increase the length and width dimensions of the cage – the larger the cage, the more space it takes up in your house. A multi-level cage, on the other hand, provides extra space by adding different levels. You can arrange your multi-level cage so that the litter pan is on the bottom with the food and resting while playing areas are on the upper floors.

No matter which option you choose, you should also think about how you are going to provide your rabbit with free space. Ideally, your rabbit should only spend a few hours a day (most likely at night) in his cage – the rest of the time he should be allowed to roam freely or given time in an open enclosure or rabbit run. To build your own rabbit run, all you need are a few interlocking mesh panels. You can also build a wooden frame and cover the sides and top with wire mesh. If you use your rabbit run outdoors, be sure to provide your rabbits with an area of shade.

d.) Chew Toys and Accessories

Netherland Dwarf Rabbits do not require a great many accessories for their cages. There are, however, a few things you may find useful in addition to the basics. The basic necessities include:

- Water Bottle

- Food Bowl(s)

- Hay Compartment

- Litter Pan

- Chew Toys

- Nest Box or Shelter

- Other Toys

Toys for Netherland Dwarf Rabbits do not need to be extravagant – they do not even need to be store-bought! You can make your own rabbit toys at home out of cardboard tubes, boxes, plastic balls, wooden blocks and whatever else you have on hand! Please ensure that any materials used are non-toxic and BPA free.

2.) Feeding Netherland Dwarf Rabbits

One of the most important things you can do to keep your Netherland Dwarf Rabbit healthy is to feed him the right diet. Most pet rabbits have similar dietary needs, but that doesn't mean that they are simple – in order to thrive, pet rabbits need a vegetable-based diet founded on healthy grasses and supplemented with commercial rabbit pellets to fill in nutritional gaps. In this section you will learn the basics about the nutritional needs of Netherland Dwarf Rabbits as well as tips for forming a healthy diet for your own pet rabbit.

a.) Types of Food for Netherland Dwarf Rabbits

The main portion of your rabbit's diet should consist of grass and hay, supplemented with commercial rabbit pellets. In addition to these staple foods, however, you can also offer your rabbit small portions of fresh fruits, vegetables and other plants. Keep in mind that certain plants can be very harmful for your Netherland Dwarf Rabbit. Before you feed your rabbit anything besides Timothy hay or pellets, you should check this list:-

<u>Plants Harmful to Rabbits:</u>

Acorns	Juniper
Aloe	Jack-in-the-Pulpit
Apple Seeds	Laurel Lupine
Almonds	Lily of the Valley
Asparagus Fern	Marigold
Azalea	Milkweed
Carnations	Mistletoe
Clematis	Nutmeg
Daffodil Bulbs	Oak
Eucalyptus	Parsnip
Fruit Pits	Poppy

Fruit Seeds	Peony
Geranium	Philodendron
Gladiola	Poinsettia
Hemlock	Rhubarb Leaves
Hyacinth Bulbs	Sweet Potato
Impatiens	Tansy
Iris	Tomato Leaves
Ivy	Tulip Bulbs
Jasmine	Violet
Jessamine	Yew

These lists are not comprehensive; in order to determine whether a specific plant is toxic for your rabbit, consult the House Rabbit Society website: http://rabbit.org/poisonous-plants/

b.) Commercial Rabbit Pellets

Do not just grab a bag of rabbit pellets off the shelf – not all rabbit pellets are created equal. It is important that you take the time to review the ingredients list on the package to determine whether it is a good quality food to offer your rabbit. Netherland Dwarf Rabbits require a diet that is low in protein and high in fiber. The majority of your rabbit's diet should be made up of high-quality feed, also called pellets. Ideally, rabbit pellets should contain no more than 16% protein and at least 15% to 20% fiber.

If you purchase a low-quality feed, you may be purchasing a product that consists mainly of feed dust or one that contains artificial "binders". You should also be sure that the feed is free from corn and growth hormones. The main ingredient in your rabbit's pellets should be alfalfa – if it is first on the ingredients list that means it is the main ingredient by concentration.

When reading the food labels on your rabbit's pellets, you should look to determine what type of grain is used. The two most commonly used grains in rabbit pellets are oats and barley. Corn is not ideal, though very small amounts in the feed are unlikely to cause any negative effect. Many Netherland Dwarfs prefer oat formulas over barley formulas but your rabbit's preferences may be different. If you want to try out different types of feed, be sure to make the transition slowly so it doesn't upset your rabbit's stomach.

In addition to commercial rabbit pellets, you can also feed your rabbits some fresh fruits and vegetables. Be careful, however, because offering rabbits too much can be detrimental, especially to young rabbits whose stomachs are still sensitive.

Food Safe for Rabbits

Apples	Orange
Beans	Pear
Blueberries	Papaya
Carrots	Pineapple
Cherries	Peach
Dandelion Greens	Peas
Grapes	Parsnip
Kale	Parsley
Mustard Greens	Raspberries
Mango	Strawberries
Melon	Tomatoes (fruit)

c.) Amount to Feed Netherland Dwarfs

Netherland Dwarf Rabbits are a small breed so they do not require as much food as other rabbits. You should keep in mind, however, that the amount you feed your Netherland Dwarf Rabbit will vary depending on its age and size. Baby rabbits that have just been weaned should be given unlimited access to pellets until they reach 6 months of age. During this time you can also offer baby rabbits Timothy hay. It is not a good idea, however, to give your baby rabbits too many vegetables because it can upset their stomachs.

Once your rabbit reaches 6 months of age you can begin feeding it a limited amount of rabbit feed. Netherland Dwarf Rabbits should be fed 0.75 to 1 oz (21.3 g to 28.3 g) of feed per pound (0.45 kg) of body weight. Netherland Dwarfs weigh an average of 2 lbs (0.91 kg) which means they need about 2 oz (56.6 g) of feed, or about ¼ cup (American), per day.

You may choose whether you want to offer all of your rabbit's food at once or if you want to divide it into two separate feedings. In addition to the pellets, you should also make sure your rabbits have an unlimited supply of Timothy hay and fresh de-chlorinated water. Don't be too worried about getting the amount of pellets exactly right – if your rabbits are still hungry, they will always have hay to eat and, if they are given too much food, they do not have to eat the extra.

d.) **General Feeding Tips for Rabbits:**

- Check your feed often for signs of mold or foul odor – these signs indicate that the feed has gone bad

- Choose a certain time of day to feed your rabbits or divide their food into two daily meals (rabbits appreciate routine)

- Trust your rabbits – if they suddenly stop eating the feed there may be something wrong with it and you should remove it immediately

- If they stop eating and it isn't the food, they may be ill, so watch them carefully and take them to the vet if you are concerned.

- Make any dietary changes slowly – drastic changes in feed can cause severe digestive problems

- Always use pellets within 60 days of manufacture (not purchase)

- Avoid commercially produced rabbit treats because they are rarely healthy

- Always keep an unlimited supply of fresh de-chlorinated water available for your rabbits – dehydration can cause severe health problems

3.) Litter Training Your Rabbit

In many cases, rabbits will litter train themselves because they are naturally clean animals. If you do need to litter train your rabbit, however, it is not difficult to do. You will need to start by isolating your rabbit in a small area without carpeting (this will make it easier to clean up any mess.

Next, prepare a litter box that is large enough for your rabbit to lie down in. Fill the litter box with about 1 inch (2.54 centimeters) of non-toxic litter and cover it with a layer of hay. If you can, take some of the soiled hay from your rabbit's cage and add it to the litter box to encourage your rabbit to use it. Confine your rabbit to the area with the litter box until he begins to urinate exclusively in the litter box.

Another option is to place multiple litter boxes in your rabbit's cage. Keep an eye on your rabbit and take note of which areas he tends to choose to do his business. Keep the litter boxes in those areas and remove the rest. Your rabbit might have a few accidents outside the litter box now and then but this is normal behavior.

**Note: Certain types of litter are harmful to Netherland Dwarf Rabbits including clay litter, clumping litter, pine or cedar shavings and corn cob litter.

Chapter Six: Keeping Healthy

** **Note:** This section may be upsetting to any children who may read it. Sadly like all our pets, Netherland Dwarf Rabbits are susceptible to developing certain health issues.

In order to keep your Netherland Dwarf Rabbit happy and healthy, you need to keep its cage clean and offer it a varied, high-quality diet. You should familiarize yourself with some of the diseases most commonly affecting this breed. If you know the symptoms and warning signs, you can quickly make a diagnosis and seek the proper treatment for your pet – the sooner you take action, the greater your rabbit's chances for making a full recovery. The details in this section are not exhaustive and not designed to take the place of a qualified veterinarian who will have up to date knowledge and information regarding current treatments for any ailments.

1.) Common Health Problems

Some of the common health problems covered in this chapter include:

- Colibacillosis
- Dental Problems
- Dermatophytosis
- Enterotoxemia
- Fleas/Mites
- Listeriosis
- Mastitis
- Myxomatosis
- Otitis Media
- Papillomatosis
- Parasites
- Pneumonia
- Rhinitis
- Uterine Cancer
- Viral Hemorrhagic Disease
- Wool Block

Colibacillosis

Colibacillosis is characterized by severe diarrhea and it is often caused by *Escherichia coli*. This disease can be seen in two forms depending on the rabbit's age. Newborn rabbits may exhibit a yellowish diarrhea – in newborns, this condition is often fatal and can affect the entire litter. In weaned rabbits, the intestines may fill with fluid and hemorrhages may surface.

In the case of weaned rabbits, the disease is typically fatal within 2 weeks. If the rabbit survives, it is likely to be stunted. Treatment is not often successful but, in mild cases, antibiotics may help. Rabbits that are severely affected with this disease should be culled to avoid the spread of the disease.

Causes: *Escherichia coli*
Symptoms: yellowish diarrhea in newborns; fluid-filled intestines and hemorrhages in weaned rabbits
Treatment: antibiotics; treatment is not often effective

Dental Problems

All rabbits, including Netherland Dwarf rabbits, are prone to developing dental problems. The most common issues are overgrown molars and enamel spurs. Your rabbit's teeth may become overgrown or develop spurs if you don't provide enough fiber-rich foods. Fibrous foods are naturally abrasive which helps to keep your rabbit's teeth filed down. In most cases, dental problems require veterinary treatment.

Causes: diet too low in fiber
Symptoms: overgrown molars, enamel spurs
Treatment: veterinary exam and treatment

Dermatophytosis

Also known as ringworm, dermatophytosis caused by either *Trichophyton mentagrophytes* or *Microsporum canis*. These infections typically result from poor husbandry or inadequate nutrition. Ringworm can be transmitted through direct contact with an infected rabbit or sharing tools such as brushes. The symptoms of ringworm include circular raised bumps on the body. The skin is these areas may be red and capped with a white, flaky material. Some of the most common treatments for ring worm include topical antifungal creams that contain miconazole or itraconazole. A 1% copper sulfate dip may also be effective.

Causes: *Trichophyton mentagrophytes* or *Microsporum canis;* typically results from poor husbandry or inadequate nutrition

Symptoms: circular raised bumps on the body; skin is red and capped with a white, flaky material

Treatment: include topical antifungal creams that contain miconazole or itraconazole; 1% copper sulfate dip

Enterotoxemia

Enterotoxemia is a disease characterized by explosive diarrhea and it typically affects rabbits between the ages of 4 and 8 weeks. Symptoms of this condition include lethargy, loss of condition and greenish-brown fecal matter around the perianal area. In many cases, this condition is fatal within 48 hours.

The primary cause of this disease is *Clostridium spiroforme*. These organisms are common in rabbits in small numbers but they can become a problem when the rabbit's diet is too low in fiber. Treatment may not be effective due to the rapid progression of the disease but adding cholestryamine or copper sulfate to the diet can help prevent enterotoxemia. Reducing stress in young rabbits and increasing fiber intake can also help.

Causes: *Clostridium spiroforme*

Symptoms: lethargy, loss of condition and greenish-brown fecal matter around the perianal area

Treatment: may not be effective; adding cholestryamine or copper sulfate to the diet can help prevent

Fleas/Mites

Indoor rabbits are unlikely to contract fleas and ticks on their own. If your rabbit spends time outside or if you have other pets that spend time outside, however, your rabbit could be at risk. Mites are typically found in the ears and fur of rabbits and they most often present themselves after your rabbit's immune system has already been compromised.

Fur mites tend to stay at the base of the neck or near the rabbit's rear. If left untreated, mites and fleas can cause severe itching, bald spots and bleeding. The best treatment for fleas and mites is a prescription medication called Revolution, known in the UK as Stronghold. Another treatment option in the UK is Ivermectin drops.

Causes: exposure to infested pets, spending time outside

Symptoms: itching, bald spots, bleeding

Treatment: prescription medication; Revolution in the USA, known in the UK as Stronghold or Ivermectin drops.

Listeriosis

Listeriosis is a type of sporadic septicemia which often causes sudden death or abortion – this condition is most common in pregnant Does. Some of the contributing factors for this disease include poor husbandry and stress. Some of the common symptoms include anorexia, depression and weight loss.

If not properly treated, the *Listeria monocytogenes* responsible for the disease can spread to the blood, liver and uterus. Treatment is not often attempted because diagnosis is not frequently made premortem.

Causes: *Listeria monocytogenes*
Symptoms: anorexia, depression and weight loss; often causes sudden death or abortion
Treatment: not often attempted because diagnosis is not frequently made premortem

Mastitis

This condition is most commonly seen in rabbitries but it can affect single rabbits. Mastitis is a condition that affects pregnant Does and it is caused by *staphylococci* bacteria. The bacteria infect the mammary glands, causing them to become hot, red and swollen. If the disease is allowed to progress, it may cause septicemia and become fatal.

Does affected by mastitis are unlikely to eat but they will crave water. The rabbit may also run a fever. Treatment for this condition may include antibiotic treatment. Penicillin, however, should be avoided because it can cause diarrhea. Kits should not be fostered because they will only end up spreading the disease.

Causes: *staphylococci* bacteria
Symptoms: hot, red and swollen mammary glands; loss of appetite; fever
Treatment: antibiotics

Myxomatosis

Myxomatosis is a viral disease that is caused by *myxoma* virus. This condition is typically fatal and it can be transmitted through direct contact or through biting insects. Some of the initial symptoms of the disease include conjunctivitis, eye discharge, listlessness, anorexia and fever. In severe cases, death may occur after only 48 hours.

Treatment for this condition is generally not effective and it can cause severe and lasting damage. A vaccine is available to be given after the rabbit reaches 6 weeks of age.

Causes: by *myxoma* virus; transmitted through direct
contact or through biting insects
Symptoms: conjunctivitis, eye discharge, listlessness,
anorexia and fever
Treatment: generally not effective; vaccine is available

Otitis Media

Also called "wry neck" or "head tilt," otitis media is caused
by an infection resulting from *P multocida* or *Encephalitozoon
cunuculi*. These bacteria cause the accumulation of fluid or
pus in the ear, causing the rabbit to tilt its head. Antibiotic
therapy may be effective, though it may just worsen the
condition. In most cases, rabbits infected with this condition
are culled.

Causes: *P multocida* or *Encephalitozoon cunuculi* bacteria
Symptoms: accumulation of fluid or pus in the ear, causing
the rabbit to tilt its head
Treatment: antibiotic therapy may be effective

Papillomatosis

Papillomatosis is fairly common in domestic rabbits and it
is caused by the *rabbit oral papillomavirus*. This disease
results in the formation of small grey nodules or warts on

the underside of the tongue or floor of the mouth. Another type, caused by *cottontail papillomavirus*, may produce horned warts on the neck, shoulders, ears and abdomen. There is no treatment for these conditions but the lesions typically go away on their own in time.

Causes: *rabbit oral papillomavirus, cottontail papillomavirus*
Symptoms: small grey nodules or warts on the underside of the tongue or floor of the mouth or horned warts on the neck, shoulders, ears and abdomen
Treatment: no treatment; the lesions typically go away on their own in time

Parasites

One of the most common parasites found in rabbits is *Encephalitozoon cuniculi*. This protozoan parasite can survive in the body for years without causing any harm. In some cases, however, the parasite can cause severe damage. This parasite typically causes nerve damage which results in head tilting, incontinence, paralysis and rupture of the lens of the eye.

Intestinal worms are also a common problem in rabbits. Both of these conditions can be treated with de-worming paste. This treatment can be used for infected rabbits and as a preventive against parasites. When used as a preventive, the paste is typically administered twice a year.

Causes: *Encephalitozoon cuniculi, intestinal worms*
Symptoms: head tilting, incontinence, paralysis and rupture of the lens of the eye
Treatment: de-worming paste

Pneumonia

Pneumonia is fairly common in domestic rabbits and it is most often a secondary infection. The most common cause of pneumonia in rabbits is *P multocida* bacteria, though other kinds may be involved. A precursor of pneumonia is often upper respiratory disease which may be a result of inadequate ventilation or sanitation.

Some of the common symptoms of pneumonia include listlessness, fever and anorexia. Once they show symptoms, most rabbits succumb to the infection within 1 week. Though antibiotic treatment is often used, it is not typically effective because it may not be administered until the disease is highly advanced.

Causes: *P multocida* bacteria
Symptoms: listlessness, fever and anorexia

Treatment: antibiotic treatment is often used but not typically effective

Rhinitis

Rhinitis is the medical term used to describe sniffling or chronic inflammation in the airway and lungs. This condition is often caused by *Pastuerella,* though *Staphylococcus* or *Streptococcus* may also be involved. The initial symptom of this disease is a thin stream of mucus flowing from the nose. As the disease progresses, the flow may encrust the fur on the paws and chest. Sneezing and coughing may also be exhibited. This condition generally resolves itself but even recovered rabbits can be carriers of the disease.

Causes: is often caused by *Pastuerella,* though *Staphylococcus* or *Streptococcus* may also be involved
Symptoms: sniffling or chronic inflammation in the airway and lungs; thin stream of mucus flowing from the nose
Treatment: generally resolves itself

Uterine Cancer

A common cause of death in female rabbits, uterine cancer can easily be prevented. Spaying female rabbits between the ages of 5 months and 2 years is the best way to prevent this disease. In un-spayed female rabbits, uterine cancer can spread to several different organs before the disease is diagnosed. At that point, treatment is typically ineffective.

Causes: tumor growing in the uterus
Symptoms: other reproductive issues; endometriosis, bulging veins, vaginal discharge, bloody urine
Treatment: spaying female rabbits to prevent; once the cancer develops, treatment is generally ineffective

Viral Hemorrhagic Disease

Also called rabbit hemorrhagic disease, viral hemorrhagic disease is caused by *rabbit calcivirus* transmitted through direct contact or contaminated food, water and bedding. Unfortunately, there is no effective treatment for this condition and many rabbits die from it without ever showing symptoms.

Some of the most common symptoms of viral hemorrhagic disease include difficulty breathing, paralysis, lethargy, bloody discharge from the nose, weight loss and convulsions. Once symptoms appear, the disease is typically fatal within 2 weeks.

Causes: *rabbit calcivirus*; transmitted through direct contact or contaminated food, water and bedding
Symptoms: difficulty breathing, paralysis, lethargy, bloody discharge from the nose, weight loss and convulsions
Treatment: no effective treatment

Wool Block

All breeds are prone to developing a dangerous condition called Wool Block although it is most prevalent in wooly breeds. Wool Block occurs when a ball of hair forms in the stomach and intestines of the rabbit, preventing it from digesting any food. This can lead to inadequate nutrition and eventual starvation and death. Rabbits are incapable of vomiting to clear the hairball. It is recommended that you speak to your breeder before purchasing your rabbit as some people feel that a pre-disposition to wool block can be inherited. You can check with your breeder whether it is a problem that they have experienced with their stock.

There are several things that you can do to help prevent and diagnose wool block. Your rabbit must have access to fresh de-chlorinated water at all times and should have lots of exercise. It is essential that your rabbit is fed with a diet that is high in fiber and contains plenty of hay. Many owners supplement with papaya tablets or fresh papaya or pineapple chunks once a week as the enzymes in these help dissolve the food within the fiber and therefore allow it to be passed more easily through the intestines. Other owners will on one day each week feed their rabbit hay and two tablespoons of whole oats and/or extra fresh vegetables. On this day, they do not feed their rabbit any pellets, allowing their stomach an opportunity to clean out. You should also ensure that your rabbit is groomed properly to reduce the amount of hair that they ingest.

Additionally you should study their droppings each day and become familiar with what is normal for your rabbit and note any changes. Droppings that become smaller or are a string of beads mixed with hair, can be a sign of wool block. Due to the seriousness of this condition, if you are in any doubt, you should seek veterinarian advice immediately.

Causes: Ball of hair in the stomach and intestines
Symptoms: Changes in eating patterns, weight loss, change in droppings, lethargy
Treatment: Seek veterinarian attention as opinions vary on treatment

2.) Preventing Illness

There are several things you can do to help protect your rabbit against disease. The most important thing is to provide your rabbit with a clean, healthy environment. It is essential that you clean your rabbit's cage on a regular basis and provide plenty of fresh de-chlorinated water for him to drink. You should also be sure to provide a healthy, varied diet that meets all of your rabbit's nutritional needs.

Dangerous/Toxic Foods

There are certain foods and plants which can be very harmful for your Netherland Dwarf Rabbit. Please refer to the list of foods that can cause serious problems in the Feeding Netherland Dwarf Rabbits section in Chapter Five. You can also check with your vet or local breeder on any local foodstuffs that you might consider feeding your rabbit to help prevent unnecessary health problems.

Recommended Vaccinations

Having your rabbit vaccinated is one of the best things you can do to protect it from disease. Two of the most important vaccines for Netherland Dwarf Rabbits are against myxomatosis and viral hemorrhagic disease (VHD) – both of these vaccinations are highly recommended. These vaccines are available as single vaccines, which need to be taken nine days apart every six months, or as a single combined vaccine once a year. The recommended vaccines for your rabbit will depend on where you live and your vet can advise you what is required.

It is a good idea to have your rabbit examined as soon as possible by a vet after you bring it home. Your vet will be able to assess your rabbit's condition and set a schedule for future check-ups. Additionally, your vet will also offer recommendations on what vaccines your pet needs and how often he needs them. This will vary from area to area so getting up to date local knowledge is essential. It may seem like a needless cost to take your rabbit to the vet once a year but it can save you a lot of money and heartache in diagnosing serious diseases before they become untreatable.

Ears, Eyes, Nails and Teeth

In addition to vaccinating your rabbit you should also check its condition on your own from time to time. Take a look inside your rabbit's ears for signs of wax buildup or infection – unpleasant odor may also be a sign of infection. Your rabbit's feet should be dry and free from sores. If you notice patches of skin where the fur has worn away or swelling, you should seek immediate veterinary care. When petting your rabbit, take the time to check its skin and coat. If you notice white flakes or tiny white dots, your rabbit could have mites or fleas.

A rabbit's nails grow continuously so you will need to trim them every six to eight weeks. Trimming your rabbit's nails is not a difficult task but it does require a degree of caution. Inside your rabbit's nail lies the quick – a vein which supplies blood to the nail. If you cut your rabbit's nails too short, you could sever the quick and induce severe bleeding. When clipping your rabbit's nails it is best to only cut off the pointed tip. To be safe, have your veterinarian show you how to properly trim a rabbit's nails before you try it yourself.

One of the most common causes of runny eyes in rabbits is a bacterial eye infection. These infections can be very dangerous and must be treated by a veterinarian as soon as possible. In many cases, antibiotics will be prescribed to handle the infection.

Obstructions and inflammation in the eye may be the result of natural or unnatural causes. In some cases, a piece of bedding or some other object may get stuck in the eye causing it to water or become inflamed. It is also possible, however, for a misshapen eyelid or part of the bone in the rabbit's face to cause an obstruction. If the flow of tears is obstructed, they may form a path down the cheek, discoloring the fur. Depending on the cause of the obstruction, surgery may be necessary to correct the issue.

If the rabbit's eyes do not produce enough tears on their own, they may become dry and irritated. When the eyes become too dry, they are more prone to scratches and erosions which can have a devastating effect on your rabbit's ability to see properly. Some of the symptoms of dry eyes include squinting, eye discharge, redness and inflammation. Trauma to the eye can also interfere with the production of tears and should be evaluated by a veterinarian.

Depending what type of litter you use in your rabbit's cage, your rabbit could develop watery eyes as a result of allergies. Dust from the litter, hay or food in your rabbit's cage can get into the eyes and cause irritation. To prevent this from happening, choose litter that is dust-free and make sure the cage is well ventilated.

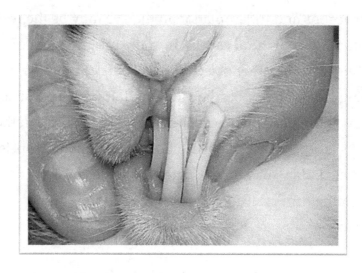

In some rabbits, the teeth are not properly aligned,
a condition called malocclusion.

If your rabbit's teeth are not properly aligned they can develop a condition called malocclusion. There are three main causes of this, the most common being genetic predisposition, injury or bacterial infection. If you provide your rabbit with adequate chew toys, you shouldn't have to worry about its teeth becoming overgrown.

You should, however, make frequent checks to see if the teeth are properly aligned – if they aren't, your rabbit could develop molar spurs or abscesses in the mouth.

3.) Pet Insurance

Many pet owners have discovered that pet insurance helps defray the costs of veterinary expenses. Pet insurance is similar to health insurance in that you pay a monthly premium and a deductible (excess in the UK) and the pet insurance pays for whatever is covered in your plan and can include annual exams and blood work. Shopping for pet insurance is similar to shopping for health insurance in the United States. As with health insurance, the age and the overall health of your rabbit will determine how much you will pay in premiums and deductibles.

Ask plenty of questions to determine the best company and plan for your needs. Some of the questions that you should ask are:

- Can you go to your regular vet, or do you have to go to a vet assigned by the pet insurance company?

- What does the insurance plan cover? Does it cover annual exams? Surgeries? Emergency illness and injury?

- Does coverage begin immediately?

- Are pre-existing conditions covered? In addition, if your rabbit develops a health issue and you later have to renew the policy, is that condition covered when you renew your policy?

- Is medication covered?

- Do you have to have pre-authorization before your pet receives treatment? What happens if your rabbit has the treatment without pre-authorization?

- Is there a lifetime maximum benefit amount? If so, how much is that amount?

Take the time to research your pet insurance options. Compare the different plans available, what each covers, and the cost before making the decision on which is best for you and your pet. Of course, pet insurance may not be the answer for everyone.

While pet insurance may not be a feasible option for you, consider having a backup plan, just in case your rabbit requires emergency care or you run into unexpected veterinarian costs.

A simple way to prepare for an emergency is to start a veterinary fund for your rabbit. Decide to put a certain amount of money aside each week, each month, or each paycheck to use in the case of an emergency. Think about the potential financial costs of veterinary care and plan for how you will pay for it now instead of waiting until something occurs.

Chapter Seven: Breeding

The following is intended as a broad overview only. If you decide to move forward with the breeding of rabbits, you will need to conduct extensive research in the process and make sure that you have all the necessary supplies on hands.
Little lives will be depending on you!

Breeding Netherland Dwarf Rabbits can be a very rewarding experience. It can also, however, be quite a challenge. Because these rabbits are so small, complications can occur with breeding so you need to be very careful. For this reason, it is incredibly important that you pick the right rabbits for breeding and that you oversee the breeding process to ensure the health and wellbeing of your rabbits. In this chapter you will learn the basics about breeding Netherland Dwarf Rabbits and caring for the young.

1.) Basic Breeding Information

As you learned in the beginning of this book, a female rabbit is called a Doe and a male is a Buck. Breeding is the process through which a male and female rabbit are mated in order to produce a litter of kits (babies). Netherland Dwarf Rabbit Does generally reach sexual maturity very early, at 3 months of age, with Bucks being one or two months later. Most breeders, however, prefer to wait until the rabbits are 6 months old to begin breeding. If you plan to breed your female rabbits, you must do so before they reach 1 year of age because this is the age at which the pelvic bones fuse – if the rabbit is not bred before this happens, it could be impossible for her to birth a live litter.

In breeding Netherland Dwarf Rabbits it is also important that you choose a pair that is not overweight. If the female is too heavy, the extra fat around her ovaries may prevent eggs from being released properly. Overweight males, on the other hand, may be less interested in breeding. To produce high-quality litters, choose a female from the same litter as a show-quality Doe and use a male of the highest quality you can afford.

A Doe's estrus (heat) cycle is so frequent that she is almost continuously capable of getting pregnant. After a Buck and a Doe have been mated, ideally, the female rabbit will become pregnant. At this point, she will enter a period of gestation – this is the length of time it takes for the babies to develop. For Netherland Dwarf Rabbits, the gestation period typically lasts about 29 to 30 days. After about 10 to 14 days of breeding you should be able to palpate the Doe to feel whether or not she is pregnant. Do this very carefully so that you do not injure the Doe or her kits. At the end of the gestation period the Doe will give birth to her kits in a process called kindling.

Once the kits have been born, the Dam (mother rabbit) will care for them. The kits will receive nutrition from their mother's milk, nursing for the next few weeks until they are old enough to be weaned. During the last two weeks of the gestation period and while your Doe is lactating, it is important that you provide her with a healthy diet higher in protein than her normal diet – this will enable her to produce enough milk to feed her kits.

2.) The Breeding Process

Before you introduce your male and female rabbits to each other, you need to be sure they are both healthy and of good breeding age. Most rabbits tend to prefer breeding in the morning and evening, so these are the best times to attempt a mating. Ideally, the female rabbit should be brought into the male rabbit's cage rather than the other way around. If you put the male in the female's cage, he may be too distracted by the strange environment to mate.

Once the Doe is ready for mating, she will stretch herself out and raise her tail. It should not take long for the male to climb on and the mating process itself takes only a few seconds. You do not need to remove the female rabbit immediately – wait a few minutes to see if the two breed again. Multiple sessions can increase the chance of pregnancy and may also increase the size of the litter.

After conception has occurred, at around day 26 or 27, it is a good idea to set up a nest box in the cage. The female rabbit will line the nest box with hay in preparation for kindling and may also pull out some of her own fur to line the nest. To build your own nest box for your Netherland Dwarf Rabbits, just construct a simple plywood box 10 x 10 x 10 inches (25.4 x 25.4 x 25.4 centimeters). If you are worried about the temperature in your home, you might want to place a specialist low-wattage lamp about 12 inches (30.5 centimeters) over the box to keep your kits warm. Heat lamps with thermostats are available in a price range of $35 to $50 (£22.75 to £32.50) with replacement bulbs averaging $10 to $15 (£6.50 to £9.75). Ensure that you get a specialist heat lamp to reduce the risk of fire.

After 29 to 30 days, the Doe will be ready to give birth. Once the birthing process begins, it is important that you stay to supervise. Netherland Dwarf Rabbits are prone to a number of birthing complications including weanling enteritis and stillborn kits. Netherland Dwarf Rabbits generally have litters of only 2 to 3 kits, though new mothers may have fewer. It is not uncommon for small breeds to produce stillborn kits, particularly during a first breeding.

The Doe may wait a few hours after birth to feed the kits, so do not be alarmed. You should check the babies after birth and remove any stillborn kits. After that, leave the babies alone for at least the first day so as not to agitate the mother. If the Doe gives birth to her kits outside the nest box, it is imperative that you move them into the nest box so they do not die of exposure. The mother rabbit will not do this on her own so it is up to you. If the kindling goes well, however, you can wait 24 hours to check on the kits.

3.) Raising the Babies

Netherland Dwarf kits are born with sealed eyes, sealed ear canals and no hair. Because they are essentially defenseless the kits need to be protected and kept warm in a nest box. Do not worry if you don't see the Dam nursing the kits frequently – feeding typically only takes about 5 minutes out of the entire day and the mother will not spend much time with the kits outside of nursing.

In case you don't see the babies feeding, check the shape of their bodies to see if they are being fed. Well-fed babies should have rounded bellies that puff out to the sides.

A day or two after birth, the kits will begin to develop a layer of fuzz which will help keep them warm. After about 10 days the kits should open their eyes and their ears should open up as well. If the eyes don't open on their own after 10 days, use a warm cloth to gently open the lids.

After this, check the kits every day to make sure the eyes do not stick shut again. After about 3 weeks, the babies generally start to sample solid food and they should be completely weaned around 5 to 6 weeks of age. Once the kits are weaned it is best to remove the mother from the cage.

You can continue to keep the kits together for another few weeks but separate them when they reach 6 to 8 weeks of age. Netherland Dwarf Rabbit Does reach sexual maturity on average at 3 months of age but can be earlier than this and for this reason it is important that you separate the sexes before they can breed.

Chapter Eight: On Show

As you've already learned, the Netherland Dwarf Rabbit is incredibly popular in show. Before you can show your own rabbits, however, you need to familiarize yourself with the breed standard to see if your rabbits comply. You should also take the time to learn a little bit about rabbit shows in general so you will be prepared for your first showing.

1.) Breed Standard

The British Rabbit Council (BRC) has set forth a standard of perfection for the Netherland Dwarf Rabbit breed that adds up to a total of 100 points. The categories covered by this standard include: body, ears, head, eyes, color, coat and condition. The breed standard also determines the faults and disqualifications for the breed.

A breakdown of the standard of points is as follows:

Body = 30 points possible

Ears = 15 points possible

Head = 15 points possible

Eyes = 5 points possible

Color = 15 points possible

Coat = 10 points possible

Condition = 10 points possible

Total = 100 points possible

Not only will you need to know the breakdown of points for the Netherland Dwarf Rabbit's breed standard, but you will also need to understand what each category means.

Below you will find an in-depth explanation of each category as it relates to the Netherland Dwarf Breed Standard:

Weight = Ideally 2 lbs (0.91 kg), disqualified if over 2.1 lbs (0.95 kg). Juniors under 6 months must weigh a minimum of 1 (0.45 kg) and less than 2 lbs (0.91 kg).

Body = (30 points possible)
Short, compact, cobby, full chested and wide shouldered. Short, straight front legs. Devoid of raciness (arch starting from the neck right down to the tail)

Ears = (15 points possible)
Erect and of good substance. Well-furred, slightly rounded at tips. Desired length 2 inches (5.08 centimeters).

Head = (15 points possible)
Round, broad skull.

Eyes = (5 points possible)
Round, bold, bright and of good color.

Color = (15 points possible)
Accept any color so long as it conforms to the normal pattern of accepted colors of other breeds.

Coat = (10 points possible)
Soft, short, dense, rollback.

Condition = (10 points possible)
Firm in flesh, good coat, free from any disease.

Faults
Ears not erect, bent ears, ears over length, narrow face, narrow shoulders, white toenails in colored rabbits, white hairs, ticking on shaded rabbits, black hairs in blue coats, fly-back coat.

Disqualifications
Crooked legs, racy type, odd colored, wall or speck eyes, white armpits, white patches, putty nose, running eyes, mutilated or maloccluded teeth, not in fit condition.

The American Rabbit Breeders Association accepts 36 showable varieties of Netherland Dwarf Rabbit. These colors are divided into 5 color groups, including:

Group 1 – Self
Blue-Eyed White (BEW)
Ruby-Eyed White (REW)
Black
Blue
Chocolate
Lilac

Group 2 – Shaded
Siamese Sable

Siamese Smoke Pearl

Sable Point

Tortoise Shell

Group 3 – Agouti
Chestnut

Opal

Chinchilla

Squirrel

Lynx

Group 4 – Tan Pattern
Otter

Silver Marten

Smoke Pearl Marten

Sable Maren

Tan

Group 5 – Any Other Variety (AOV)
Broken

Fawn

Himalayan

Orange

Steel

The ARBA also uses a slightly different schedule of points than the BRC. The breakdown of points is as follows:

Body (Conformation or Type) = 35 points possible

Head = 15 points possible

Ears = 15 points possible

Eyes = 5 points possible

Fur = 10 points possible

Color = 15 points possible

Condition = 5 points possible

Total = 100 points possible

2.) What to Know Before Showing

The key to success in rabbit shows is to be prepared. This involves making sure your rabbit meets the breed standard and arranging the rabbit properly for judging. You should also prepare yourself by bringing along an emergency kit, just in case.

Included in your emergency kit should be:

- Nail clippers – for emergency nail trimming

- Antibiotic ointment

- Band-Aids – for minor injuries to self, not rabbit

- Hydrogen peroxide – for cleaning injuries and spots on white coats

- Slicker brush – to smooth rough coats

- Black felt-tip pen

- Business cards

- Paper towels – because you never know

- Scrap carpet square – for last-minute grooming

- Collapsible stool – when chairs are not available

- Extra clothes

- Supplies for your rabbits

3.) Tips for Finding a Show in Your Area

Finding rabbit shows in your area is not difficult if you know where to look. In most cases, you can find a list of shows on the ARBA or BRC website. You might also try the website for the New England Netherland Dwarf Rabbit Club. The links for these sites are below:

ARBA Sanctioned Shows: www.arba.net/showsSearch.php

The BRC Show Diary: www.thebrc.org/shows-current-year.htm

New England Netherland Dwarf Rabbit Club, 2013 Sanctioned Shows: www.nendrc.com/2013-sanctioned-shows.html

Chapter Nine: Care Sheet

In this chapter you will find summaries of all the Netherland Dwarf Rabbit facts that we have discussed. Included in these summaries is valuable information about the breed itself as well as cage requirements, nutritional needs and breeding information. In addition, you will also learn some valuable tips for handling your rabbit, dealing with shedding and introducing your rabbit to your children.

1.) Basic Information

Species: domestic rabbit, (Oryctolagus cuniculus)

Classification: dwarf breed

Weight: 1.1 to 3.5 lbs (0.5 kg to 1.59 kg)

Body Shape: short, compact and rounded

Body Structure: cobby, full-chested and wide-shouldered

Coat: soft, short and dense

Coat Color: 36 show colors accepted by ARBA, divided into 5 groups

Ears: erect, up to 2 inches long (5.08 centimeters)

Diet: herbivorous

Foods: commercial rabbit pellets, Timothy hay, vegetables and fruits

Supplements: generally not required if the diet is sufficient in fiber and protein

Lifespan: average 5 to 10 years

2.) Cage Set-up Guide

Location Options: indoors or outdoors

Cage Types: single-level, multi-level, open pen

Cage Materials: metal cage with wire mesh sides, solid bottom

Bedding: non-toxic pellets, fresh hay, newspaper

Accessories: water bottle, food bowls, hay compartment, litter pan, chew toys and shelter

3.) Feeding Guide

Diet Basics: low protein, high fiber

Main Diet: high-quality alfalfa pellets

Nutritional Breakdown: 16% or less protein, at least 15% to 20% fiber

Ingredients to Avoid: corn, binders, feed dust

Supplemental Foods: Timothy hay, fresh fruits, fresh vegetables

Amount to Feed: 0.75 to 1 oz (21.3 to 28.3 g) pellets per pound (0.45 kg) bodyweight, unlimited hay, and small portion of fruit/vegetable daily

Other Needs: unlimited supply of fresh de-chlorinated water

4.) Breeding Information Summary

Sexually Mature (Doe): 3 months average

Sexually Mature (Buck): 4 to 5 months average

Breeding Age: after 6 months, before 12 months

Litter Size: 1 to 2 (first breeding); 2 to 3 average

Gestation Period: lasts about 29 to 30 days

Eyes and Ears Open: about 10 days

Solid Food: begin sampling around 3 weeks

Weaning: around 5 to 6 weeks

5.) General Rabbit Care Tips

In this section you will find a number of tips regarding general rabbit care. You will find information about how to properly handle a rabbit and how to introduce it to children. You will also learn about shedding in rabbits and other general tips.

a.) Holding Your Rabbit

It is important to remember that Netherland Dwarf Rabbits are fragile creatures so you need to use caution when handling them. The first thing you need to know is that you must never pick up your rabbit by the ears. When you first bring your rabbit home you should give it a day or two to get used to the new environment before you try to hold it.

When you feel your rabbit is ready, offer it a few treats to encourage the rabbit to approach you on its own. Once your rabbit approaches you, begin petting it gently on the back and ears. If your rabbit responds well to this treatment you can try picking it up. Make sure to support your rabbit's feet and hold the rabbit's body against your chest. Do not let very young children handle the rabbit and be careful when putting it back down.

You should also know that while many rabbit breeds including the Netherland Dwarf are very friendly by nature, they generally do not like being picked up and held. Being held high off the ground can be frightening for a rabbit, so it is best to enjoy their company on the floor at your rabbit's level. You will have to judge based on your rabbits temperament and preferences.

b.) Introducing Your Rabbit to Children

Netherland Dwarf Rabbits are a very gentle breed so they have the capacity to get along with children. If your children are not properly educated in how to handle the rabbit however, it could result in accidental injury. Before you bring your rabbit home, make sure to talk to your children about the responsibilities of their new pet. Teach your children how to properly hold the rabbit and warn them that the rabbit might be frightened by loud noises. Once you bring your rabbit home, give it time to acclimate to its new surroundings. After your rabbit has become comfortable at home you can try introducing it to your kids. If it is happy for you to do so, hold the rabbit securely in your arms and let your child pet it gently. If your rabbit is calm, you can try setting it down on the ground so your child can pet it. Do not let your children pick the rabbit up unless they are old enough to know how to do so properly.

c.) Shedding in Rabbits

Some rabbits shed more than others but most breeds shed every three months. Like cats, rabbits are very clean animals and they like to groom themselves. Unlike cats, however, rabbits cannot vomit – thus, if they consume too much hair it could form a ball in the stomach and cause serious health problems. Please see Chapter Six regarding keeping healthy for more information regarding wool block.

For this reason, it is essential that you brush your rabbit at least once a week to remove loose and dead hairs from its coat. During shedding seasons, you may need to brush Netherland Dwarf Rabbits once a day or even multiple times a day to keep up.

6.) Planning for the Unexpected

If something happens to you, you want to know that your rabbit and any other pets will be properly cared for and loved. Some cell phones allow you to input an ICE (In Case of Emergency) number with notes. If your cell phone has such an option, use it. If it does not, write the following information on a piece of a paper and put it in your wallet with your driver's license:

- The names of each of your pets, including your rabbit.

- The names and phone numbers of family members or friends who have agreed to

temporarily care for your pets in an
emergency.

- The name and phone number of your
veterinarian.

Be sure to also talk with your neighbors, letting them know
how many pets you have and the type of pets. That way, if
something happens to you, they can alert the authorities,
ensuring your pets do not linger for days before they are
found.

If you fail to do that and something happens to you,
someone will find your rabbit and any other pets and will
need to know what to do to ensure that they are cared for.
It is a good idea in the case of an emergency, to ask several
friends or family members to be responsible for taking care
of your pets should something happen to you. Prepare
instructions for the intended guardians, providing
amended instructions as necessary. Also, if you are happy
to do so, be sure to provide each individual with a key to
your home (remember to inform your home insurance
company so that this does not affect your coverage).

Instructions should include:

- The name and phone numbers of each individual who agreed to take care of your rabbit and other pets.

- Your pet's diet and feeding schedule.

- The name and phone number of your veterinarian.

- Any health problems and medications your rabbit may take on a daily basis, including dosage instructions, instructions on how to give the medicine, and where the medicine is kept.

Put as much information as necessary to ensure the guardians can provide the same level of care to which your rabbit is accustomed.

Chapter Ten: General Care Questions

If you have never owned a rabbit before, you may be prone to making some of the same mistakes other novice rabbit owners make. In this chapter you will learn about some of the most common myths and misunderstandings new rabbit owners face so you can avoid them yourself – you will also learn some of the mistakes inexperienced rabbit owners make so as to ensure that you don't fall into the same trap.

The Type of Bedding You Use Doesn't Matter

FALSE

Choosing the right type of bedding is very important for Netherland Dwarf Rabbits. Certain kinds of bedding can get stuck in their coats. For this reason, you should avoid using shavings as bedding. A better option is to use straw or hay. When purchasing bedding, be sure it is non-toxic and fresh – you should also shake off as much dust as possible before using the bedding in your rabbit cage being careful not to breath in the dust.

You Should Never Feed Your Rabbit Grass

FALSE

There is a common myth that feeding your rabbit grass will cause bloat and/or diarrhea. In reality, grass can actually be good for your rabbit! After all, wild rabbits eat a diet that consists primarily of grass, right? You do, however, need to be careful about letting your rabbit munch on the grass in your yard. If you use fertilizers, pesticides or other chemical lawn treatments it could be dangerous for your rabbit. As an alternative, try growing a pot or container of grass for your rabbit indoors using only organic ingredients.

You Can Feed Rabbits any Type of Vegetable
FALSE

The food you offer your Netherland Dwarf Rabbits has a direct impact on their health. You probably already understand the importance of eating the right foods for your own health, so it should be easy to see how the same is true of pet rabbits. Rabbits are herbivores by nature so they should not be feed any meat-based foods.

The main component of a Netherland Dwarf Rabbit's diet should be grass hay like Timothy or meadow hay. You can also supplement your rabbit's diet with legume hay, fresh vegetables and commercial rabbit pellets. Do not assume that if you only give your rabbit commercial pellets he will be healthy – these pellets are not enough to give your rabbit the nutrition he requires.

Some rabbit owners also make the mistake of making changes in their rabbit's diet too quickly. Rabbits have very delicate digestive systems so any changes to their diets must be made slowly. Juvenile rabbits should not be fed vegetables while their digestive systems are still developing. Once they reach maturity, however, you can slowly begin introducing vegetables and then may offer them a variety of vegetables on a daily basis.

You Should Never Feed Your Rabbit Fruit

FALSE

This myth is founded on the idea that feeding rabbit fruit or other sweet foods encourages the growth of bacteria. While refined sugars are most certainly not ideal for rabbits to eat, natural sugars (fructose) like those found in fruit are perfectly okay. In fact, grass and hay naturally contain some of this sugar anyway.

You Can Keep Males and Females Together

FALSE

Inexperienced rabbit owners sometimes fail to understand just how quickly and how often rabbits are capable of breeding. A female rabbit's estrus (heat) cycle is so frequent that she is almost continuously capable of getting pregnant. This is an important fact to keep in mind when keeping male and female rabbits in the same cage.

Many rabbit owners encounter unwanted breeding when they fail to separate the sexes early enough. Though female rabbits generally reach sexual maturity around 3 months of age and males around 4 to 5 months, they are capable of breeding as early as 2 months. To avoid unwanted breeding, it is essential that you separate the sexes before that point.

This is most likely to happen after a new litter is born. If you do not have experience keeping or breeding rabbits, you may not expect rabbits from the same litter to breed so readily. If you allow rabbits from the same litter to breed it can result in inbreeding and genetic defects. You shouldn't even keep male and female rabbits in the same cage if you want them to breed – outside a period of time long enough for them to mate, after which point the female should be removed from the cage.

Rabbits Need to be Kept in Pairs
FALSE

If you perform some basic research on keeping rabbits as pets you are likely to find a number of resources claiming that rabbits need to be kept in pairs or they might become "lonely". Keep in mind that "lonely" is a human emotion – rabbits do not have human feelings. As long as you provide your rabbit with plenty of attention and human interaction, it will be perfectly fine on its own.

You Should Pick Your Rabbit up Often
FALSE

While many rabbit breeds including the Netherland Dwarf are very friendly by nature, they generally do not like being picked up and held. Being held high off the ground can be frightening for a rabbit, so it is best to enjoy their company on the floor at your rabbit's level.

I Don't Need to Have My Rabbit Examined by a Vet
FALSE

Routine veterinary care is important. It is recommended that you vaccinate your rabbit against Myxomatosis and Viral Hemorrhagic Disease (VHD). It is also often required for getting pet insurance, holiday boarding and attending events. After reading the health section of this book you should know that many rabbit diseases progress rapidly, often without showing any symptoms. This being the case, taking your rabbit to the vet once or twice a year may be the only way to help catch diseases before they progress beyond repair.

Pet Rabbits Belong Outdoors
<u>FALSE</u>

There are benefits to keeping a rabbit outdoors but you should think carefully before you do so. Some rabbit owners claim that rabbits should ONLY be kept outdoors while others claim that indoors is best. The choice is ultimately yours to make but keep in mind that outdoor rabbits are more likely to be exposed to disease, inclement weather and extreme temperatures. They may also not get as much attention as indoor rabbits which could affect their temperament and overall well-being.

Chapter Eleven: Frequently Asked Questions

When you first buy a Netherland Dwarf Rabbit, you are likely to have questions. In this chapter you will find answers to some of the most frequently asked questions regarding these rabbits. Some of the topics covered in this section include:

- General Care for Rabbits
- Buying Netherland Dwarfs
- Housing Netherland Dwarf Rabbits
- Feeding Netherland Dwarfs
- Breeding Netherland Dwarf Rabbits
- Health Concerns for Netherland Dwarfs

Q: What precautions should I take when buying from a breeder?

A: You should take the same precautions in buying from a breeder as you would in a pet store or shelter. You will need to examine the individual rabbits to make sure they are healthy before you even begin to talk about purchasing one. In addition to checking the health of the stock, you should also determine the breeder's experience and credentials. Ask the breeder questions to determine how much they know about the breed, how much experience they have and whether or not they have the required license or registration to breed rabbits legally.

Q: Is it okay to buy Netherland Dwarf Rabbits from online ads?

A: Purchasing any animals from an online ad is risky for a number of reasons. First, you will not be able to view the animal before purchase to make sure that it is in good condition. Second, by buying online it will mean that the animal will have to be shipped. The shipping process can be extremely stressful and dangerous for animals because they may be exposed to extreme temperatures and rough handling. Please avoid buying animals online.

Q: Should I buy one Netherland Dwarf Rabbit or two?

A: The answer to this question has many variables. If you are a new rabbit owner, you may find it easier to care for one rabbit than to care for two. If you really think about it, however, caring for two rabbits is not a significant amount more work than caring for one – you can keep them both in the same cage and offer them the same food. You should also consider the fact that Netherland Dwarf Rabbits are friendly, social creatures and they enjoy the company of other rabbits. It is best to keep these rabbits in pairs or groups of three but they can be kept alone if provided with enough care and attention. Please remember that if you try to keep two rabbits together and one is more dominant than the other, the subservient rabbit could become stressed and fall ill due to the bullying of the other rabbit. If you truly want to form a close bond with your rabbit, it is best to keep only one. Your rabbit doesn't need another rabbit companion as long as you give it plenty of love and attention yourself. In fact, your rabbit is more likely to bond with you if you do not keep it with another rabbit. If, however, you do want to keep more than one rabbit together it is best to buy them when they are the same age so they can be raised together. It is not a good idea to add a new rabbit to an already established cage – this is likely to cause territorial issues.

Q: What kinds of costs should I be prepared for?

A: Netherland Dwarf Rabbit owners are responsible for a number of costs, some of which recur on a monthly basis. When you are just getting started you will need to cover the costs for the rabbit cage and accessories as well as the rabbit itself, having it spayed or neutered and microchipped. After setting up the cage and buying the rabbit, you will then need to purchase food and bedding on a monthly basis. You should also be prepared to cover additional costs for veterinary care and replacement items.

Q: Can Netherland Dwarf Rabbits be kept outside?

A: Pet rabbits can generally be kept outside in a hutch but you should think carefully before choosing this option. Rabbits that are kept outside are more likely to be exposed to disease and there is also the risk of predators getting into the cage and harming or killing your rabbits. Keeping your rabbits outdoors may also mean that you do not pay as much attention to them as you would if they were indoors – for this reason, it is essential that outdoor rabbits be kept in pairs or trios.

Q: What are the benefits of adopting an adult rabbit?

A: Many people prefer to buy baby rabbits because they want to raise the rabbit themselves. While this is a wonderful experience, there are also several unique benefits involved in adopting an adult rabbit. Adult rabbits are more likely to already be litter trained which will save you the hassle of having to do it yourself. It is also more likely that the rabbit will already be spayed or neutered because this is a policy most shelters enforce. Adopting an adult rabbit may also be a little cheaper than buying a baby rabbit from a pet store or breeder. If you adopt a rabbit from a shelter, you also have the added benefit of giving a loving home to a rabbit that needs one.

Q: Can I build my own rabbit cage?

A: Yes, you can build your own rabbit cage as long as you use the appropriate materials and make it the right size. The easiest way to make your own rabbit cage is to use stackable wire cubes to create a multi-level cage. Insert wooden dowels through the gaps to create supports for wooden shelves and line the shelves with towels to make them more comfortable for your rabbit. Make sure that any sharp edges are fled away or covered to avoid injury.

Q: Can I let my rabbit play outside?

A: Yes, you can let your rabbit play outside as long as you take a few precautions. First, it is important that your rabbit receives all the necessary vaccinations to keep him protected against disease. Second, you should build or buy an outdoor rabbit run that will keep your rabbit safe while he is outside. Even while your rabbit is confined to the run you should keep an eye on him.

Q: **How big should my rabbit cage be?**
A: In response to this question, many experienced rabbit owners will reply "the bigger the better." At minimum, however, your rabbit cage should be wide enough for your rabbit to stretch all the way out. The cage should be about four times your rabbit's size in length. Keeping your rabbit in a cage too small can result in health problems.

Q: **How often should I clean my rabbit's cage?**
A: The best answer to this question is "as often as necessary". If you have multiple rabbits in one cage, you may need to clean out the cage more often than you would for a single rabbit. Generally, you should plan to change your rabbit's bedding once a week but you may need to clean the litter box two or three times within that same period of time.

Q: At what age can I begin breeding my Netherland Dwarf Rabbits?

A: Netherland Dwarf Rabbit Does can typically reach sexual maturity as early as 3 months of age. Breeders however generally wait until the female rabbit is considered sexually mature for breeding at 5-6 months while males are generally considered sexually mature at 6 months.

Q: Can't I just keep a male and female in the same cage together if I want to breed them?

A: Keeping male and female rabbits together in the same cage will result in breeding, but it may not be a healthy situation for your rabbits. After a female rabbit becomes pregnant, she will enter a 29-30 day gestation period. During that time it is not possible for the female to become pregnant again but the male may continue to attempt to breed. This can be exhausting for the female rabbit and dangerous if the male becomes aggressive in his advances. It is best to separate the sexes after breeding to ensure that the female rabbit is able to rest and the babies develop properly.

Q: Should I worry if the Dam doesn't begin feeding the babies right away?

A: No. It is not uncommon for Netherland Dwarf Rabbit Dams to wait a day or two before they begin feeding their young. If she has not begun feeding them after two days, however, you may want to consider using a foster mother. If you introduce the litter to a foster mother while they are young enough, she will be less likely to reject them.

Q: Will I need a license if I plan to breed my Netherland Dwarf Rabbits?

A: The answer to this question varies depending where you live. In most cases, a license is not required for individuals to keep Netherland Dwarf Rabbits as pets. If you live in the United States of America and plan to breed your rabbits, however, you may need to obtain a license. A license is not required in the U.K. to breed rabbits, however. Be sure to check with your local council to find the answer to this question.

Q: Do I need to give my rabbit supplements?

A: As long as you provide your Netherland Dwarf Rabbits with a healthy, varied diet you should not need to give them any supplements. Giving your rabbits supplements is, however, an option and it can help to boost their nutrition.

One suggestion is to provide your rabbit with a salt or mineral block. In addition to giving your rabbits iodine and other minerals, it can also help relieve their boredom. Small (teaspoon size) pieces of fruit such as banana, apple, oatmeal or herbs can be used as treats but should only be given occasionally. Do not give your rabbits any human food or vitamin supplements without checking with your veterinarian first.

Q: Should I refill my rabbit's bowl of pellets during the day?

A: No. If you keep refilling your rabbit's bowl, your rabbit may eat more of the pellets than hay. Hay and vegetables are the most important parts of your rabbit's daily diet so you should do what you can to encourage him to eat those foods. Commercial pellets are a supplement to your rabbit's diet of hay and vegetables.

Q: What vaccinations are required for my rabbit?

A: Vaccinations are not required but certain ones are highly recommended. The two most important vaccines for rabbits are against myxomatosis and viral hemorrhagic disease (VHD). Both of these diseases are very serious and often fatal. Aside from preventive vaccination, treatments for these diseases are typically ineffective.

Q: Do I need to have my rabbit examined by a vet?

A: Again, it is your choice whether or not you provide your rabbit with routine veterinary care. Some rabbit owners prefer to save themselves the expense of veterinary visits while others see the value in it. The benefit of taking your rabbit in for regular check-ups is that you can catch diseases and conditions in the early stages and provide treatment. You can also keep your rabbit up to date on recommended vaccinations.

Q: What are the health benefits of spaying/neutering?

A: Some rabbits exhibit behavioral changes if they are not spayed or neutered - they may become more aggressive and they may spray urine. For female rabbits, spaying greatly reduces the risk for uterine cancer. Uterine cancer is one of the most common causes of death in un-spayed rabbits and it is often untreatable by the time a diagnosis is made. Neutering male rabbits will help prevent them from fighting with other rabbits which could also serve to extend their lives. It is best to discuss the advantages and disadvantages with your vet.

Chapter Twelve: Relevant Websites

When you start looking around the internet it can take some time to track down exactly what you are looking for.

Shopping

A one-stop shop for all your rabbit needs is what is required and the sites below offer you the convenience of pulling together many of the best products from around the web. Enjoy Shopping!

United States of America Website
www.rabbitsorbunnies.com

United Kingdom Website
www.rabbitsorbunnies.co.uk

In this chapter you will find a relevant websites for useful information in the following categories:

Food for Netherland Dwarf Rabbits

Care for Netherland Dwarf Rabbits

Health Information for Netherland Dwarf Rabbits

General Information for Netherland Dwarf Rabbits

Showing Netherland Dwarf Rabbits

1.) Food for Netherland Dwarf Rabbits

These websites will provide you with a wealth of information that you will need to know about feeding your Netherland Dwarf Rabbits a healthy diet. You will receive information about your rabbit's nutritional needs, food options and more.

United States of America Websites:

"Feeding Your Rabbit the Correct Way."
www.rabbitmatters.com/feeding-your-rabbit.html

Logsdon, Alexandra. "Feeding Your Pet Bunny for a Long Healthy Life." Zooh Corner.
www.mybunny.org/info/rabbit_nutrition.htm

"Feeding Instructions." Sherwood Forest Natural Rabbit Food.
www.naturalrabbitfood.com/feeding-instructions

United Kingdom Websites:

"Basic Dietary Guidelines for a Healthy Netherland Dwarf Rabbit." Dee Millen Rabbits.
www.netherlanddwarfrabbit.co.uk/5.html

"Rabbit – Facts and Care Sheet." Freshfields Animal Rescue.
www.freshfieldsrescue.org.uk/images/uploads/articles/Rab bit_care_sheet1.pdf

"Feeding Pet Rabbits." Woodward Veterinary Practices.
www.woodward-vets.co.uk/information/Feeding%20Pet%20Rabbits.pdf

2.) Care for Netherland Dwarf Rabbits

The websites in this section will provide you with great information regarding caring for Netherland Dwarf Rabbits. You will find information regarding housing and raising rabbits as well as tips for purchasing a rabbit from a breeder.

United States of America Websites:

"Netherland Dwarf Rabbit Care and Info." New England. Netherland Dwarf Rabbit Club. www.nendrc.com/netherland-dwarf-rabbit-care-and-info.html

"Caring for Your Netherland Dwarf." New Hampshire Netherlands. www.nhnetherlands.com/caring-for-your-netherland-dwarf.html

"Care of Netherland Dwarf Rabbits." LovetoKnow Small Pets. http://small-pets.lovetoknow.com/care-netherland-dwarf-rabbits

"Care of Netherland Dwarf Rabbits." Raising-Rabbits.com. www.raising-rabbits.com/care-of-netherland-dwarf-rabbits.html

United Kingdom Websites:

"Housing for Your Rabbit." Dee Millen Rabbits. www.netherlanddwarfrabbit.co.uk/6.html

"Rabbits." The Royal Society for the Prevention of Cruelty
to Animals.

www.rspca.org.uk/allaboutanimals/pets/rabbits

"Care for Your Rabbits." DutchRabbits.co.uk.

www.dutch-rabbits.co.uk/care.html

"Rabbit Care." The Royal School of Veterinary Studies.

www.ed.ac.uk/polopoly_fs/1.37142!/filemanager/rabbit%20
care.pdf

3.) Health Information

The websites in this section will provide you with a wealth
of information to help you keep your Netherland Dwarf
Rabbits healthy. You will find information about common
health problems, vaccinations and other health-related
information.

United States of America Websites:

"Choosing a Netherland Dwarf Rabbit." PetPlace.com.
www.petplace.com/small-mammals/choosing-a-
netherland-dwarf-rabbit/page1.aspx

"Rabbit Health – With Proper Care Rabbits Make Charming Companions." RabbitMatters.com.

www.rabbitmatters.com/rabbitcare.html

"Parasitic Diseases of Rabbits." The Merck Veterinary Manual.

www.merckmanuals.com/vet/exotic_and_laboratory_animals/rabbits/parasitic_diseases_of_rabbits.html

United Kingdom Websites:

"Netherland Dwarf Rabbit Breed Guide." ClickPets.co.uk.

www.clickpets.co.uk/advice/netherland-dwarf-rabbit-breed-guide/125

"Health." The People's Dispensary for Sick Animals.

www.pdsa.org.uk/pet-health-advice/rabbits/health

"Bunny Care." Dee Mill Rabbits.

www.netherlanddwarfrabbit.co.uk/5.html

4.) General Information

The following websites will provide you with general information about Netherland Dwarf Rabbits – here you will find information regarding the history of the Netherland Dwarf breed, general facts and owner testimonials.

United States of America Websites:

"Netherland Dwarf Rabbits." Courtney's Critters. www.courtneyscritters.com/netherlanddwarfrabbits

"The Netherland Dwarf Rabbit." RabbitMatters.com. www.rabbitmatters.com/netherlanddwarf.html

"Raising Rabbits – The Basics." DebMark Rabbit Education Resource. www.debmark.com/rabbits/basics.htm

United Kingdom Websites:

National Netherland Dwarf Rabbit Club. www.nndrc.co.uk/

"Rabbit – Netherland Dwarf Breed Profile." PetPlanet.co.uk. www.petplanet.co.uk/small_breed_profile.asp?sbid=10

Bethel Bunnies. www.bethelbunnies.co.uk

5.) Showing Netherland Dwarf Rabbits

The following websites will provide you with some of the information you need to know about showing Netherland Dwarf Rabbits in either the U.S.A. or the U.K. You will find information regarding the breed standard, how points are awarded and how to prepare for shows.

United States of America Websites:

"Netherland Dwarf Rabbit Standard." New England Netherland Dwarf Rabbit Club,

www.nendrc.com/netherland-dwarf-rabbit-standard.html

"Showing Your Netherland Dwarf Rabbit." New Hampshire Netherlands.

www.nhnetherlands.com/showing-your-dwarf.html

"What to Take to a Rabbit Show." New England Netherland Dwarf Rabbit Club,

www.nendrc.com/what-to-take-to-a-rabbit-show.html

United Kingdom Websites:

"Netherland Dwarf Standard." Dee Millen Rabbits.
www.netherlanddwarfrabbit.co.uk/2.html

"Breed Standard." National Netherland Dwarf Rabbit Club.
www.nndrc.co.uk/#/breed-standard/4549007486

"Breed Standard of the Netherland Dwarf." Scottish
Netherland Dwarf Rabbit Club.
www.scottishnetherlanddwarf.co.uk/Breed%20Standard.ht
m

Index

Index

Index

Index

spayed or neutered 15, 21, 111, 112, 117

stillborn kits 81

T

teeth 27, 29, 36, 57, 71, 73, 74, 87

temperament 29, 96, 107

time considerations 26

Timothy hay.. 46, 49, 51, 93, 94, 103

travel carrier 22

treats 52, 96, 116

U

Uterine Cancer.. 55, 65, 66, 117

V

vaccinations... 20, 21, 22, 23, 32, 69, 70, 112, 116, 117, 123

vegetables 24, 46, 48, 50, 68, 93, 94, 103, 104, 116

vet/veterinarian..21

22, 25, 31, 33, 51, 55, 68, 69, 70, 71, 72, 73, 75, 76, 99, 100, 107, 116, 117

veterinary care 20, 22, 24, 25, 71, 76, 107, 111, 117

Viral Hemorrhagic Disease.. 55, 66, 69, 107, 116

W

water 26, 51, 52, 61, 66, 67, 69, 72, 94

water bottle... 22, 26, 44, 94

watery eyes 73

weaned 49, 56, 79, 83

weight..9, 50, 60, 66, 67, 68, 86, 93

wild rabbits 10, 102

Wool Block.. 55, 67, 68, 98

Index

Index

Photo Credits

Cover Design:- Liliana Gonzalez Garcia, ipublicidades.com (info@ipublicidades.com)

Title Page Photo by Yuki Matsukura (Flickr: Netherland dwarf) via Wikimedia Commons http://commons.wikimedia.org/wiki/File:Netherlands_dwarf_rabbit.jpg

Page 1 Photo by Ranveig via Wikimedia Commons http://commons.wikimedia.org/wiki/File:Young_Netherland_Dwarf_rabbit.jpg

Page 5 Photo by SloMo2639 [Public domain], via Wikimedia Commons http://commons.wikimedia.org/wiki/File:Strider-Netherland_Dwarf_Rabbit.JPG

Page 11 Photo by shogun1192 GPL via Wikimedia Commons http://commons.wikimedia.org/wiki/File:Netherlandwarf.jpg

Page 14 Photo by Flickr user Matsubokkuri

www.flickr.com/photos/matsubokkuri/3125502474/sizes/l/in/photostream/

Page 20 Photo by Muriel Gottrop via Wikimedia Commons

http://commons.wikimedia.org/wiki/File:Netherlanddwarfbunny.jpg

Page 30 Photo by Flickr user Matsubokkuri

www.flickr.com/photos/matsubokkuri/3117801146/sizes/l/in/photostream/

Page 35 Photo by Flickr user Twdelish

www.flickr.com/photos/ann_white/5265451997/sizes/m/in/photostream/

Page 37 Photo by Flickr user Matsubokkuri

www.flickr.com/photos/matsubokkuri/2775533046/sizes/l/in/photostream/

Page 43 Photo by Flickr user Matsubokkuri

www.flickr.com/photos/matsubokkuri/2775517602/sizes/l/in/photostream/

Page 50 Photo by Erebus555 at en.wikipedia
http://commons.wikimedia.org/wiki/File:Netherland_Dwar
f_On_Brick.jpg

Page 53 Photo by Lauri Rantala (originally posted to Flickr
as Höpö), via Wikimedia Commons
http://commons.wikimedia.org/wiki/File:H%C3%B6p%C3
%B6_Netherland_Dwarf.jpg

Page 54 Photo by Rebeccabrown1982 [Public domain], via
Wikimedia Commons
http://commons.wikimedia.org/wiki/File:Paul_the_baby_bu
nny_rabbit.JPG

Page 70 Photo by Shogun1192 [Public domain], via
Wikimedia Commons
http://commons.wikimedia.org/wiki/File:HI3A0028.jpg

Page 73 Photo by Uwe Gille
http://commons.wikimedia.org/wiki/File:Bradygnathia-
superior-rabbit.jpg

Page 77 Photo by BigStockPhoto Photo by kitkana
http://www.bigstockphoto.com/image-34425692/stock-
photo-netherlands-dwarf-rabbit

Page 82 Photo by BDK via Wikimedia Commons
http://commons.wikimedia.org/wiki/File:Baby_rabbit_nest.j
pg

Page 84 Photo by Yuki Matsukura (Flickr: Netherland
dwarf), via Wikimedia Commons
http://commons.wikimedia.org/wiki/File:Netherlands_dwa
rf_rabbit.jpg

Page 92 Photo by Shadow48576 via Wikimedia Commons
http://commons.wikimedia.org/wiki/File:Blue-
Eyed_White_Netherland_Dwarf.jpg

Page 95 Photo by Flickr user Benimoto Netherland Dwarf
black otter
www.flickr.com/photos/benimoto/2830383315/sizes/l/in/ph
otostream/

Page 101 Photo by SloMo2639 [Public domain], via
Wikimedia Commons
http://commons.wikimedia.org/wiki/File:Netherland_Dwar
f_Bunny-Strider.JPG

Page 104 Photo by Flickr user Matsubokkuri

www.flickr.com/photos/matsubokkuri/3124674125/sizes/l/i
n/photostream/

Page 108 Photo by Flickr user Matsubokkuri

www.flickr.com/photos/matsubokkuri/3117803140/sizes/l/i
n/photostream/

Page 118 Photo courtesy of: -

www.rabbitsorbunnies.com

Page 119 Photo by Flickr user Duchessoftea

www.flickr.com/photos/duchessoftea/1496373593/sizes/z/in
/photostream/

Page 127 Photo by Rhinokitty at en.wikipedia

http://commons.wikimedia.org/wiki/File%3ANetherland_d
warf_rabbit_chibi.JPG

References

Activity 8 – Breeding your Market Rabbits.
http://florida4h.org/projects/rabbits/MarketRabbits/Activity
8_Maturity.html

Bethel Bunnies. www.bethelbunnies.co.uk/

"Breed Standard." National Netherland Dwarf Rabbit Club.
www.nndrc.co.uk/#/breed-standard/4549007486

"Breed Standard of the Netherland Dwarf." Scottish
Netherland Dwarf Rabbit Club.
www.scottishnetherlanddwarf.co.uk/Breed%20Standard.ht
m

"Can I have a pet rabbit?" Department of Agriculture,
Fisheries and Forestry Biosecurity Queensland
http://www.daff.qld.gov.au/__data/assets/pdf_file/0009/577
80/IPA-Keeping-Rabbits-As-Pets-PA15.pdf

"Care of Netherland Dwarf Rabbits." LovetoKnow Small
Pets. http://small-pets.lovetoknow.com/care-netherland-
dwarf-rabbits

"Care of Netherland Dwarf Rabbits." Raising-Rabbits.com. www.raising-rabbits.com/care-of-netherland-dwarf-rabbits.html

"Caring for Your Netherland Dwarf." New Hampshire Netherlands. www.nhnetherlands.com/caring-for-your-netherland-dwarf.html

"Feeding the Angora Rabbit & Wool Block Prevention." Avillion Farm. http://avillionfarm.com/pdflib/RabbitFeedAndWB.pdf

National Netherland Dwarf Rabbit Club. www.nndrc.co.uk/

"Netherland Dwarf Rabbit Care and Info." New England. Netherland Dwarf Rabbit Club. www.nendrc.com/netherland-dwarf-rabbit-care-and-info.html

"Netherland Dwarf Rabbits." Courtney's Critters. www.courtneyscritters.com/netherlanddwarfrabbits

Netherland Dwarf Rabbits "The Gem of the Fancy".
http://www.nendrc.com/netherland-dwarf-rabbit-care-and-info.html

"Netherland Dwarf Rabbit Standard." New England
Netherland Dwarf Rabbit Club,
www.nendrc.com/netherland-dwarf-rabbit-standard.html

"Netherland Dwarf Standard." Dee Millen Rabbits.
www.netherlanddwarfrabbit.co.uk/2.html

"Rabbit – Netherland Dwarf Breed Profile."
PetPlanet.co.uk.
www.petplanet.co.uk/small_breed_profile.asp?sbid=10

"Rabbit Show Information." Rabbit Association of
Singapore. http://rabbitsingapore.org/Rabbit%20Show%20Information%20(published).pdf

"Showing Your Netherland Dwarf Rabbit." New
Hampshire Netherlands.
www.nhnetherlands.com/showing-your-dwarf.html

The Mad Hatter's Rabbitry

http://themadhattersrabbitry.weebly.com/netherland-dwarf-info.html

"The Netherland Dwarf Rabbit." RabbitMatters.com.

www.rabbitmatters.com/netherlanddwarf.html

Three Little Ladies Rabbitry

http://www.threelittleladiesrabbitry.com/woolblock.php

"What to Take to a Rabbit Show." New England Netherland Dwarf Rabbit Club

www.nendrc.com/what-to-take-to-a-rabbit-show.html

CPSIA information can be obtained
at www.ICGtesting.com
Printed in the USA
BVHW071327170620
581539BV00006B/486